LIGHT IN A DARK PLACE

PLACE

The Prison Years

Darryl Robert Schoon

This book is dedicated

TO THE MEMORY OF MY PARENTS

AND

TO THE FUTURE OF OUR CHILDREN.

Special thanks to
Martha, my wife
Marshall, my friend
Penny Cooper and Chris Arguedas, my attorneys
&
To all those who love and support me
I know who you are and you do too

FOREWORD

From the beginning of our friendship in law school, Darryl has stretched my limits, his unique perspective constantly challenging my reality. Darryl's voice is one that at times seems to tap into the very soul of the universe. It is a voice I am grateful to have known and one I am proud to recommend. Throughout the years, the space of love, appreciation and gratitude are present whenever I have interacted with Darryl. This book presents an opportunity for you to experience the same.

Marshall Thurber

The birds moved as one then hesitating dove like a family of acrobats at home with each other in the tent of their universe towards the telephone wires ahead and there they lit with the grace immanent in nature and in their selves for me to watch with the awe of one condemned to never fly except in dreams and maybe also in thoughts of release it occurred to me that if I were a bird I not knowing the harmony of which I were a part would crash instead into others and then become lost going north as they went south or vice versa but you do know what I mean here don't you who listen to these words like birds on wing searching for the polestars of your being in a universe so vast as to make you homesick for a home you can't remember and now can only hope might exist somewhere somewhere somewhere...But isn't it true that if I were a bird I would like them be also free?

How can you know
What is true
When the world reflects
Only what you think

Judgments
Tautological foundations of time
Observations
Ontological moments in eternity

ASSIGNED SEATING

In the summer of 1986 I received a phone call from Penny Cooper, my attorney, telling me she had to see me as soon as possible. The feds had just made an offer and she wanted to discuss it before replying. I had been working at a gold mine in Nevada waiting for my criminal case to come to resolution and this might be it. So, I drove to Reno, flew to the Bay Area, and went to see Penny.

She wasn't happy and neither would be I. Their offer, she said, could hardly be called that. In return for my guilty plea, the feds would recommend a sentence of fifteen years. Penny said she couldn't in good conscience recommend their offer. I concurred. It was as if in return for my promising to stand still, they would only shoot below my waist.

I called to reserve a seat on the next flight to Reno. They were fully booked so I had to fly United. At the time, it was the only other airline that flew to Reno from San Francisco and I had an intense dislike for United. Their corporate image was too close to that of the red, white, and blue, an organization I had been at odds with since the 1960s. They had only a few seats left and I had to take what was assigned.

Boarding the plane, I saw an attractive woman on that about to be filled flight. I glanced at my ticket. My assigned seat was the one next to hers. Not in the best mood, I made a negative comment as my carry-on barely fit under the seat in front me. I still remember her reply, "Don't worry, there's always a rainbow behind every cloud." And, although I wasn't inclined to agree, there was merit to what she said.

She asked if I worked in Nevada, and I said that I was currently working at a gold mine. I asked her the same question. She said she was a prostitute working at the Kit Kat. I was floored. The flight was full. It was assigned seating. And I was sitting next to an attractive woman who had just told me she was a prostitute at one of the better houses in Nevada. Although I was still in deep trouble with the law I knew this latest turn of events was evidence again of the ineffable presence of God.

We had a wonderful conversation on the flight back. She was very much into positive thinking, and because her profession was one that lent itself to the suspension of judgment I told her of the predicament I was currently facing. As accepting of my profession as I was of hers, she repeated once again, with sincere conviction, that behind every dark cloud there was a rainbow.

We talked about many things, and the conversation turned to her current boyfriend who she said worked at the Kit Kat as a driver and helper. He was a paraplegic and somewhat insecure about her affection for him, given his physical condition and her profession. She said, though, she truly loved him, adding, "He shouldn't worry. He's got a great tongue."

We landed sooner than I expected, her presence and the nature of the conversation making the time pass by quickly. She said goodbye and as she stepped into the waiting area, I saw her boyfriend. What I remember is not that he was in a wheelchair, though he was. What I remember is the look on his face when he saw her, a look of total love. And she was right. There is a rainbow behind every cloud. But that was something I wouldn't be sure of until several years later.

2

———————

I've seen the streets of Shanghai
The souks of Marrakech
The alleyways of Tangiers
The forbidden ways of flesh

Had White House invitations
I've years in prison done
I've seen my share of trouble
I've had my share of fun

And I've learned the world's not
What it seems to be
For the ways of men and women
Are filled with mystery

That the Great Unknown which fills them
With fears of every kind
Are simply misconceptions
Of the growing human mind

That if you stop and listen
To the promptings of your heart
You'll find you're taken care of
By He who's done his part

For the love that He has given
Is still here on the earth
Waiting for the Christ inside
To be given birth

———————

Observing
The judgments
As they pass right on through

Attempting
To tell me
What's false and what's true

Caught
By my thinking
And the webs that they spin

Seeing
At long last
The trap I've been in

Holding
To the center
Of all that is true

Now free
From the bindings
Of all that I knew

I thank YOU
My dear SELF
For the gift of this sight

For
At long last and finally
I know it's all right

MY ROAD DOG MOW

road dog, prison slang for a close friend in the joint

My road dog at Lompoc was an unusual one. He, like I, was Chinese. Unlike myself, he was in his late sixties, in excellent physical shape. I was in my early forties. But as a drug dealer, my daily routine had included numerous phone calls and restaurants, not physical exercise. But in more ways than one those days were over and, as if to emphasize the point, the day I met Mow, he took me out onto the track and we walked for four miles. The four miles per day regimen would continue uninterrupted for two years until he was released. The next day, it ceased.

I found Mow's case an interesting one. In the eyes of the U.S. government, Mow was in prison for possession of heroin with intent to sell. In my eyes, Mow was in prison for being Chinese. In his sixty plus years of life, Mow had never once used heroin, let alone sell it or any other drug for that matter. In fact, Mow didn't smoke or drink. His one vice had been gambling, and to the Chinese gambling is not a vice. It is simply a cultural pastime. Unfortunately, for Mow, it was to be, at least indirectly, the reason he would end up in prison

After retiring, Mow had opened a gambling operation. Knowing Mow, it was safe, clean, and honestly run, something that can't be said for a lot of establishments, legal or otherwise, these days. Mow's tastes and needs were simple. He didn't need a big house or a fancy car, he just liked gambling and the gambling world; and, as a result, now had some extra money. This extra money, too, was to be, also, indirectly, a reason Mow was to end up in prison.

One of Mow's relatives, hearing of Mow's improved economic status, had approached Mow for a down payment on a house. Mow had given it, and because it was later found out the relative had a heroin habit, Mow had found himself with a bad debt. And, since it was a relative, and since money did not mean to Mow what it meant to a bank or mortgage company, Mow just considered himself out of luck—how out of luck he would eventually find out.

But just when Mow decided the money was gone forever, he received a phone call from his relative saying he now had a way to pay Mow back. And although he didn't actually have the money, he did have a plan. The problem was it was the police who had come up with the plan, not his relative. Unbeknownst to Mow, his relative's plan was to give Mow to the police instead of himself after being arrested for possession of heroin.

5

The police plan was simple. Mow's relative would tell Mow the plan was to buy and sell some heroin and with the proceeds pay Mow back. Having both a buyer and a seller, all he needed was a loan to first purchase the heroin. The police then recorded the phone call and when Mow agreed to the loan, immediately arrested Mow. Now, I would say Mow was guilty of having a worthless relative, of having made two bad loans, of wanting to be repaid, and of living in a land with unjust laws. The U.S. government, however, says Mow is a heroin dealer and they have the conviction to prove it.

And although I am sorry for Mow's unfortunate experience with the law, I am, and will be forever grateful for having known him, even under such adverse conditions. Mow had an unflinching spirit, an ever present curiosity, and integrity uncommon to these times, let alone the place. Prison gave me many gifts. One of them was a road dog named Mow.

Sometimes it seems that life's a battle
Sometime it seems it's one big war
Sometimes then, I will wonder
How much longer, how much more

I don't know why it's so crazy
Why it seems to have no aim
And that's the time I'll ask the question
Where's the lesson in this pain

I see people hope tomorrow
Will be better than today
I see people hope that hoping
Somehow'll drive the pain away

I don't know why it's so crazy
Why it seems to have no aim
And that's the time I'll ask the question
Where's the lesson in this pain

I keep hoping love is real
And not what it seems to be
A trap in which the lonely falter
A treasure box without a key

I don't know why it's so crazy
Why it seems to have no aim
And that's the time I'll ask the question
Where's the lesson in this pain

(Austin Songwriters Contest, lyrics, 2005 3rd Place)

———————

A foolish man thinks
A wise man knows
A fool becomes a wise man
When he knows that
A wise man becomes a
Fool when he thinks

———————

I think
Therefore I forget that
I AM THAT I AM

———————

Thought
Gives rise to
The idea of self

The idea of self
Gives rise to
The idea of aloneness

The idea of aloneness
Gives rise to
Fear in the world

Treasure thought and your treasure is fear in the world
Treasure life and your treasure is love in the world

THIRION'S TALE
PART I

Some stories are only told under certain circumstances, when certain events lead to the telling. Otherwise those stories would never be told and would, of course, then never be heard. This is one of those stories.

My ten-year prison sentence began in the fall of 1986 at Lompoc Federal Prison Camp in Lompoc, California. New surroundings always lead to new acquaintances. This is as true for prison as it is for other locales, only the types you meet there are different.

Dr. Norman Bernard Thirion and I would never have met on the outside. Thirion had served as international banker to Howard Hughes and had been the financial director and project planner for Archisystems, Hughes' personal holding company. Later, he was to work with Adnan Kashoggi, the flamboyant Saudi oil wheeler-dealer through whom he was to develop close ties with the Saudi royal family. My life instead had included countless phone booths from which calls could not be easily traced, and to me words like acid and coke had completely different meanings from those that Thirion thought them to have.

What we did share was an interest in business and money, and countless walks on the prison grounds were spent in discussing projects Thirion intended to pursue once he was released. Unlike

8

myself, Thirion believed himself innocent and thought that when his appeal was heard he would be freed. Unfortunately, it wasn't to happen. But because it didn't, Thirion was to tell me a story I am sure he never intended to tell anyone.

It was March 1987 when Thirion learned his appeal had been denied. That evening he took me to his room, where he showed me various documents and told me of events he believed were the reason he had been sent to prison. He then asked if I would write down his story and keep copies of certain documents for safekeeping. Thirion had a plan and said he needed the story in the hands of a third party to insure his safety.

The first document Thirion showed me was a letter of introduction from a New York movie production company, Transglobal Productions Ltd. The letter, written in 1983, was from Transglobal vice-president Perry Morgan to Lord Cranbourne, a British Viscount.

The letter to Lord Cranbourne introduced Thirion as former international banker to Howard Hughes and stated Thirion was representing Transglobal Productions in securing financing. The letter was copied to two persons, Dr. [Norman] Bernard Thirion and General Robert E. Cushman, Jr. Thirion informed me that General Cushman was not only Transglobal's Chairman of the Board, but was also retired Commandant of the U.S. Marine Corps and past Deputy Director of the CIA.

What was a former Deputy Director of the CIA doing as chairman of a movie production company? The answer: not to produce movies. Transglobal Productions never made a movie during its short existence. It did, however, successfully solicit hundreds of millions of dollars from the Saudi royal family for an Afghan government-in-exile that never received the money.

Thirion said in 1982 he had been approached by Transglobal's two vice presidents, Perry Morgan and Dr. Jon Speller. Morgan and Speller knew of Thirion's close ties to the Saudis and wanted his help in soliciting the royal family to support the Afghan resistance against Soviet invaders. They also said some of the money was to produce a movie Morgan had written.

Thirion said he was dubious about such an odd proposition, but, as a banker, he had heard many unlikely proposals. He told them he would approach the Saudi royal family for a fee of 2% of the moneys raised. Speller and Morgan agreed and, soon thereafter, Thirion said, events began to move forward quickly.

He was soon introduced to Dr. Nake Kamrany, a professor at the University of Southern California. Dr. Kamrany, a supporter of the Afghan cause, believed a government-in-exile should be created prior to asking the Saudis for money. He also believed former King Zahir Shah could provide the rallying point for the new government. To this end, Dr. Miskanyar, a former Afghan ambassador, flew to Italy to ask Zahir Shah if he would head the new organization. There, he reported, the king agreed to do so provided it received official U.S. recognition.

To Thirion, this presented a problem; how was this newly proposed organization to get official U.S. recognition? Transglobal vice-president Perry Morgan told him not to worry, stating "General Cushman was directly wired into the National Security Council; the guys at the NSC work for Cushman."

The National Security Council is the forum where the highest national security concerns are discussed for the benefit of the President of the United States. Thirion was about to discover just how close Transglobal Productions was to the Presidency itself.

In the fall of 1982, Perry Morgan asked Thirion to meet him for lunch at the Beverly Hills Hotel. There, Morgan introduced him to William Wilson, the wealthy personal confidant of President Reagan, and Personal Envoy of the President to the Vatican in Rome.

Thirion remembered wondering what William Wilson and Perry Morgan were doing together. Morgan was an entrepreneur, a hustler type, and had little in common with Wilson, an older man of substantial wealth with a direct line to the President, and, yet, they were having lunch at the exclusive Polo Lounge in Beverly Hills. Thirion did not have long to wonder. Within weeks, Thirion said he was to discover Wilson's true role in the unfolding series of events involving Transglobal Productions and the Saudi money.

Morgan's admonition not to worry about U.S. recognition was soon justified. William Clark, head of the National Security Council, informed Thirion and Dr. Kamrany that the Afghan government-in-exile would officially receive U.S. recognition. Clark told Thirion and Dr. Kamrany to fly to Rome where they would meet William Wilson. There, they would receive Wilson's assurances on behalf of President Reagan and would be given further instructions on how to proceed.

It was here Thirion again began to wonder about William Wilson. Wilson had no official connection to Transglobal yet he seemed to be everywhere, interfacing at the White House, interacting with the National Security Council, even informing Thirion he was keeping President Reagan abreast on what was happening. He told Thirion President Reagan wanted "to know more", that the President had requested Wilson to accompany him back to his ranch in Santa Barbara over Thanksgiving to "fill him in on all the details."

It was then Thirion asked Perry Morgan, "What exactly is Wilson's angle in all of this?" Perry Morgan replied:

"Wilson? Hell, he's getting $10 million for himself and $10 million for the President's retirement."

Morgan's memorable reply explained not only Wilson's role, it also explained why official U.S recognition of the Afghan government-in-exile was so easily forthcoming from powerful bodies such as the National Security Council and the Reagan White House. William Wilson, General Robert E. Cushman, and others were apparently actively engaged in a conspiracy to solicit and embezzle Saudi funds using Transglobal Productions as a cover to do so.

The proposal to the Saudi royal family by General Cushman was to be specifically described as a "private effort". This was important because there are laws prohibiting public servants from skimming public moneys. General Robert E. Cushman and others incorporated Transglobal Productions, a private corporation, as part of a conspiracy to attempt to evade the intent of such laws.

As public officials, if William Wilson or General Cushman wanted to ask the Saudis to support the Afghan resistance, either could have done so with a single phone call. Diplomatically, they were members of America's ruling elite. Instead, they created a private company through which they approached a private banker to privately solicit the Saudi funds. Believing, then, the Saudi money would be private, the conspirators thought they could legally divert the money to themselves, an erroneous legal assumption.

The belief that private activity legitimizes illegal actions was not uncommon at the Reagan White House. General Richard Secord, a participant in the Iran-Contra scandal, testified before the U.S. Senate that White House Counsel had assured him that his activities, if private, were within the purview of the law.

White House Counsel's advice notwithstanding, private actions are in no way a dispensation for legal culpability especially when there exists a prior criminal intent and conspiracy to act in violation of the law. In fact, giving such advice in itself can be construed as an overt act that qualifies as part of such a conspiracy.

Thirion and Dr. Kamrany next flew to Rome where they met Wilson in his offices at the Vatican. Wilson assured them the proposed Afghan government-in-exile had the support of President Reagan and would receive official U.S. recognition. He also informed Kamrany and Thirion he would personally convey this message to King Zahir Shah.

King Zahir Shah then announced in Paris, in June 1983, his intention to form a government-in-exile. With Zahir Shah's announcement, Thirion was now prepared to formally present his proposal to the Saudis. Already, they had expressed interest in contributing $500 million. Thirion's 2%, $10 million fee from this initially improbable venture now appeared to be within reach.

Thirion phoned Prince Abdullah, the son of Saudi Crown Prince Abdullah, to tell him of the proposal. He then had his partner, E.T. Barwick, Chairman of E.T. Barwick, a Fortune 500 Company, hand deliver it to the Prince in Atlanta. Prince Abdullah, after examining the request, gave his approval and informed Barwick that he would notify his father, Crown Prince Abdullah, brother of King Fahd, of Thirion's proposal.

The response of the Saudis was decidedly positive and Barwick phoned Thirion to tell him the news. The Saudis then asked that the financial proposal be presented to the Saudi Ambassador in Washington D.C., who would deliver it to King Fahd.

It was here events began to unravel. General Cushman called Thirion, informing him Transglobal director Rabbi Morton Rosenthal had arranged for the purchase of captured Russian-made Syrian arms from the Israelis. The arms were to be resold to the Afghan resistance, with Transglobal making a substantial profit in the middle. Cushman had expected Thirion, ever the banker, to approve, but Thirion's reaction was anything but approving.

"You're going to do what?" Thirion replied, stunned at Cushman's unexpected revelation. "If the Saudis find out we bought arms from the Israelis with their money, all hell will break loose!"

Thirion knew full well the Saudis' negative feelings about Israel. Not wanting to betray the Saudis, Thirion demanded Cushman not purchase the weapons and Cushman assured Thirion he wouldn't. But Cushman lied. Instead, Cushman decided to go ahead and cut Thirion out of the deal. This, Thirion would not discover until it was too late.

The Saudi proposal was to be presented on December 19, 1983 in Washington D.C. to Saudi Ambassador Prince Bandar. Those scheduled to attend were William Wilson, General Cushman, and E.T. Barwick, Thirion's partner.

The evening before the meeting, Wilson called Barwick and asked to meet him at the Watergate Hotel. There, Wilson told Barwick, due to a scheduling conflict, he, Wilson, would not be present at the meeting. He also told Barwick he had already met with Prince Bandar earlier that day.

The next day, General Cushman and Perry Morgan arrived at Barwick's suite. Cushman took Thirion's proposal and had Morgan retype pages four and five. It now emphasized (1), the project was "private" in nature, and (2), the group was headed by General Cushman.

After the proposal was formally presented to Prince Bandar, Barwick phoned Thirion, who was in Europe, to report that Wilson had met with Prince Bandar prior to the meeting and that Perry Morgan, at Cushman's direction, had changed the proposal. Barwick also told Thirion that Perry Morgan said Kamrany agreed to give William Wilson a fee of $10 million.

Thirion now suspected Wilson and Cushman were trying to cut him and Barwick out of their $10 million fee. His suspicions were correct. Shortly thereafter, Thirion received a letter from Cushman, notifying Thirion he was being replaced as Transglobal's financial representative by Ronald Sablosky. The letter was hand-delivered to Thirion in Europe by Ronald Sablosky himself.

Ronald Sablosky, Transglobal's new banker, was someone Thirion knew well. Sablosky had been Thirion's partner in his oil dealings with the Saudis and had intimate knowledge of Thirion's close ties to the Saudi royal family. Thirion now discovered Sablosky was also Perry Morgan's stepbrother.

Thirion tried to warn the Saudis that two brothers, Perry Morgan and Ronald Sablosky, both Jewish, were attempting to divert the money, but it was too late. Rumors were circulating that the Saudis had already transferred the funds, but where were they? The *Banque Francais de Commerce Exterieur*, Thirion's designated bank of deposit in Paris, had not received the money nor had the Afghan Government-In-Exile, the intended beneficiaries, received anything.

Thirion asked Saudi Prince Abdullah if the Saudis had transferred the funds. The Prince, after inquiring, told Thirion to have Zahir Shah, the former king of Afghanistan, call his father, King Fahd. When Zahir Shah called, King Fahd told Zahir Shah, "I am honored to have been able to have been of assistance to my Moslem brethren. The money has been sent through the Saudi Ambassador in Washington D.C. to an account controlled by the CIA in Switzerland."

Thirion's $10 million 2% fee would never be paid and the U.S. Government, one year later, would charge Thirion with accepting illegal loan fees, extradite him from Monaco, and would sentence him to five years in federal prison — a charge Thirion firmly believed was trumped up by those in the Reagan White House to discredit him should he reveal what had happened. Thirion, protesting his innocence, upon conviction immediately filed an appeal.

It was to be two years later in March 1987 when Thirion's appeal was denied that I was asked to write his story for safekeeping. Thirion had a plan to gain his release from prison, and events in the press had now confirmed elements of Thirion's extraordinary tale.

Three months previous, on December 4, 1986, the Los Angeles Times reported proceeds from the Iran-Contra arms deal had been discovered in a secret CIA Swiss bank account, <u>a bank account that also contained $500 million of Saudi and U.S. funds intended for the Afghan resistance</u>.

"Part of millions paid by Iran for U.S. made weapons was deposited in a $500 million CIA-managed bank account secretly used by the United States and Saudi Arabia to buy arms for the anti Soviet Afghan resistance. The account in question includes $250 million in deposits from both the United States and Saudi Arabia that are used to buy Soviet bloc weapons for distribution to resistance forces battling the Soviet occupation of Afghanistan."

The Los Angeles Times article confirmed not only Thirion's story but it also confirmed General Cushman and Rabbi Rosenthal had purchased the Soviet arms from Israel and resold them to the Afghan resistance. The Times article additionally raised an even more interesting question. It stated the fund was composed of $250 million contributed by the U.S. and $250 million from Saudi Arabia. Had Wilson and Cushman received the $500 million in Saudi funds solicited by Thirion, then replaced $250 million of the Saudi money with U.S. government funds and embezzled the remaining Saudi $250 million for themselves and the President?

The Afghan government-in-exile was never to receive any of the money solicited on its behalf. Three weeks after the secret CIA Swiss bank account was revealed, Dr. Kamrany, in a L.A. Times article, *U.S Aid fails to reach Afghan Fighters,* asked about the money meant for the Afghan government-in-exile:

"Where does it go? Who gets it? Why doesn't the United States ask what happened to it?"

Three months later, Newsweek Magazine, on March 23, 1987, reported:

"Word is beginning to get out in Washington that millions of dollars worth of aid intended for the freedom fighters cannot be accounted for...and last week an investigator for the General Accounting Office, the auditing arm of Congress, began to look into the allegations that aid meant for the mujahedin had been diverted on a scale that could make Ollie North look like a piker."

I was stunned. The General Accounting Office had now discovered that large amounts of money meant for the Afghan resistance had been diverted from government accounts, apparently confirming the embezzlement by the Reagan White House of the Saudi funds.

I wondered what Thirion was going to do. As Thirion had requested, I had written down his version of the events that had transpired between himself and Transglobal Productions and others. I then put away the papers for safekeeping and waited for Thirion's next move. It would surprise even me.

MOTHER EARTH

A planet spun around a sun
Its crust broke out in fire
Its oceans seethed with nitrogen
Its mountains pushed up higher

Not yet alive but being born
In the hour of its birth
Was a life that feeds us all
A life we now call earth

So many years we cannot say
She struggled to become
A planet fair and beautiful
And chose to not succumb

To the empty cold surrounding her
Lifeless empty space
For she knew that deep within her
She was to mother the human race

Her atmosphere she purified
She covered herself with plants
With flowers birds and changing clouds
She invented nature's dance

And at long long last she was ready
For her part in God's great plan
To nurture and sustain
A race to be known as man

For thousands of years she fed him
With fishes from her seas

Rice and wheat from her fertile fields
Fruits from her many trees

And man was truly grateful
In those early early days
He thanked the Mother often
And was respectful of her ways

But now he has forgotten
The gifts he does receive
He thinks they're of his doing
But himself he does deceive

Mother Earth is in deep trouble
And she needs to find a way
To survive what we have done to her
We've a debt we need to pay

We treat the ocean like a toilet
The air is dirty gray
The fish are dying from chemicals
But you know they have no say

Fish don't vote they have no power
Neither do the trees
The atmosphere has no guns
Mother Earth is on her knees

We cover her with cement
Burn a hole in her blue sky
The weather's acting crazy
And still we wonder why

Technology it will save us
Or so the scientists say
But it's technology that has caused
Most problems here today

It seems a crime is happening
Against Mother Earth herself
Is there no one to protect her
Is there no one who will help

I know the earth is dying
And I know she wants to live
But unless we act now quickly
She won't be there for us to give

Mother Earth is in deep trouble
And she needs to find a way
To survive what we have done to her
We've a debt we need to pay

———————

Denials ancient and embedded
Give way to living waters
Rushing and swelling the parched soil of self
Ah, fecund and fertile, what am I to become?

———————

As the peppers burned my mouth and throat, I thought a baby, if experiencing the same, would believe itself in danger. So, too, do we learn to enjoy experiences once thought to be threatening and uncomfortable. Aloneness in its own way brings its own pleasures.

———————

Joy
Though solitary
Is always shared

And love
Though always shared
Is also solitary

––––––––––

Suckered into adversity
Succored while there

––––––––––

MEDITATION INSIDE AND INSIGHTS CIRCA 1988

In 1986 when I started my prison sentence, my life changed forever. For one thing, I began to meditate regularly. Because of my surroundings, meditation became a retreat, a way to withdraw daily from where I now found myself. Where it would take me, I had no idea. But I meditated not because of where I wanted to go, I meditated because of where I wanted to leave.

I had been in prison for two and a half years when I wrote down in 1988 some of the thoughts that follow. I kept those writings to myself. Much like a journal, they were private in nature, personal benchmarks on my journey. And, it was not to be until eleven years later that I was to remember what I had then experienced.

In December 1999, my friend, Marshall Thurber, asked that I read Eckhart Tolle's "The Power of Now" and give him my feedback. In reading Eckhart's extraordinary book, I realized the similarities between the realities of which Eckhart Tolle wrote and that which I had experienced eleven years before. And, although I was only drinking from the waters in which Eckhart is immersed, there was no doubt the waters came from the same well.

––––––––––

If it is true, and it is, that being judgmental has been like a second nature to me; the question becomes, what, then, is my first?

---

*The quest is
To be
In a world
That is not
What it seems to be
That is the quest*

---

*Believing myself to be temporal
Led to the fear of the eternal.*

---

*Watch out!
Watch out!
This clay is awakening.*

---

*From a battle-scarred encampment
To a fountain of living waters
From one besieged by many
To one now joined to all
How long it took
Yet how quick it happened*

The ETERNAL changes or does it?
And if it doesn't then why does it seem to?

I AM WE ARE the FATHER the SON

Relieved of a task
That was never mine
Free, at last,
The life divine

I would not have any thought that would limit YOU for I would wish
to experience YOU without limits.

Great Suspectations
life before LIFE

Yes
YOU have come
When I have called

YOU have answered
When I have asked

YOU ARE
Therefore
I AM

Yes
Yes
Yes

––––––––

Younger, I contemplated sex without guilt.
Older, I contemplated life without guilt
The rest followed

––––––––

It is not impossible to be who we are
It is possible, though, to eventually cease being who we are not

––––––––

Simplicity is not austerity. It is simply Nature in her fullness.

––––––––

Within
Without
Even if there is a difference
I'm sure we don't understand

––––––––

Being blessed doesn't mean it's easy.
But, then again, it is easier being blessed.

I never expected ETERNITY to be like this. But, then again, I didn't expect time to be what it was either.

I AM
the Will's
SELF

The Oneness, as presence, both manifest and unmanifest, was there for me to see

I said to IT, to everything in particular:
"We are here together, YOU as I"

"ALL IS ME, YOU as I"
IT replied the next day

I would have my mind create only the promptings of my heart.

Seeking
Searching

Ending
Finding

The soul's ascension
The self's release

Restful knowing
The soul embracing

& I

I?
Yes
Oh Yes
At long last

I

PRISON BLUES PRISON DREAMS

In my office at home, hung on the wall is a series of framed memorabilia. Between the envelope addressed to myself from The White House and the invitation from President Carter to attend the special performance honoring the 1979 visit of the Vice-Premier of China, Deng Xiao-Ping, is a framed letter from the U.S. Department of Justice thanking me for volunteering 300 hours as a projectionist at the prison movie theater. But the one piece of memorabilia I am most proud of is a small simple poster announcing the appearance of The Blues Rockers with Willie Myers on lead guitar and harmonica, with myself and others, appearing June 19, 1991 at the auditorium at Terminal Island Federal Penitentiary.

Proving that prison is a place where dreams can still come true, I played piano with Mr. Myers in that prison blues band. I had no idea that I even had a dream to play keyboard in a blues band with someone the likes of Mr. Myers. How could I have even dreamed that dream when I had been born with a tin ear? And my deep appreciation for the blues had come the hard way. It had taken a long stretch in prison for me to truly learn to love and appreciate the slow heartfelt sounds of authentic Mississippi delta blues.

I clearly remember the day and the moment. It was on a weekend and I had just stepped out onto the north yard when I heard it — the lingering sound of a guitar note that hung in the air like longing itself before disappearing into the next chord change. I crossed the yard to the auditorium, opened the door and saw on stage the person who had played that guitar note. That was the first time I saw Mr. Myers.

Behind him were a drummer, a bass player, and a rhythm guitarist. And next to them was an old upright piano. There was no one on it and as they continued to play I moved up onto the stage and asked the rhythm guitarist what key they were in. Then I sat down at the piano and moved along with them into the familiar blues progression.

Willie Myers was the real thing and it wasn't just because he was from Indianola, Mississippi, which he was. It was simply because that's who he was. Later, after he had asked me to join the band, we had been rehearsing and the band had begun to rock out on a B.B. King number. It seemed a natural thing to do for most of us had spent time in a rock'n roll band or two. I noticed, though, that Mr. Myers had quietly put down his guitar and as we continued to play, he moved over to where I was and simply said, "B.B. didn't write it like that and I ain't gonna play it like that."

The concert we played that June 19, 1991 will be with me forever. The auditorium was packed as the word had gone out that Mr. Myers and his blues band was to perform. I was one of the few "non-brothers", i.e. racially not black, in that room and I can still feel it, playing before an overflow audience that appreciated the blues perhaps as few audiences could. We ended with a blues shuffle and as we played and the audience cheered and clapped, Mr. Myers strolled out of the auditorium before returning to play one last encore.

I don't know what Mr. Myers was in prison for. I heard it had something to do with drugs. But whatever it was, it was just another excuse white society uses to imprison and punish black men. If the drug had been tobacco and he was white, he might instead have been a corporate executive with stock options and a donor to the Republican Party which would protect his right to sell a white man's sanctioned but still lethal drug to anyone 18 years or older. But Mr. Myers wasn't white. He was black, and, as such, his rights weren't protected in a white man's society. There was a reason he played the blues the way he did.

LET 'EM RAGE

If your heart is hurt and aching
If your soul is in despair
Don't push your feelings ever deeper
Give 'em air give 'em air

If the terror's pushing upwards
If your fear's crying for release
Then accept what you are feeling
Give your feelings some relief

If you want to calm the troubled waters
Let 'em rage let 'em rage
If you want to calm the troubled waters
Let 'em rage

You can pretend to be ignorant
You can say it just ain't so
You can say that Jesus loves you
You can say you're in control

You can lie to GOD and others
You can lie to friends and kin
But lying cannot change
What you're feeling deep within

You can hide in alcohol
In pleasure or a job
But hiding's just denial
And it's you yourself you rob

'Cause if you stopped and listened
To your feelings deep inside
You'd find the love you're seeking
The love you've tried to hide

So if your heart is hurt and aching
If your soul is in despair
Don't push your feelings ever deeper
Give 'em air give 'em air

If you want to calm the troubled waters
Let 'em rage let 'em rage
If you want to calm the troubled waters
Let 'em rage

It is said that it is harder for a rich man to enter heaven than it is for a camel to pass through the eye of a needle. Verily, it is so. For there the rich man cannot take his riches, the poor man his poverty, the religious man his piety, nor the full man his pride. There, one enters clothed only in one's SELF. But verily I say unto you, your SELF is nothing less than the true cloak of Christ.

May thine I be single

DOING TIME IN THE STUDIO

In my third year at Lompoc Federal Prison Camp, a recording studio was built and I began writing lyrics, some of which were put to song. Lompoc Prison Camp was one of those places the media couldn't seem to keep away from. Stories about the "soft" conditions at Lompoc would air regularly. Any emotion is fair game for the media to exploit and taxpayer resentment is pretty much a sure bet. A shot of a tennis court in prison guarantees that result; and if a single tennis court could cause a camera crew and newsman to make the journey to Lompoc, CA, just think what the known presence of a recording studio would have done. Fortunately, some things in prison are never discovered.

The studio was the brainchild of an inmate, a genius of sorts. He was the kind of guy who would have won the science award in grammar school. In the old days, people like him never ended up in prison. But he too was to become a part of that great diaspora from the Haight-Ashbury, a scattering of the tribe to parts unknown, known, and well known. And he, like myself, was to end up at Lompoc Prison Camp, one of the better known scattering sites of the diaspora in the 1980s.

I watched as a small room in the gymnasium was transformed into a recording studio over a period of months. Walls were covered with baffled foam, and a drum machine, a complete drum set, a Fender guitar, an electric bass, a keyboard, a mixing board, and a small 4-track recording deck were combined into something quite wonderful. The prison administration was satisfied that on a very small budget, a significant addition to the camp's recreation facilities had been added.

I wrote a number of lyrics over the next few years. And I remember being amazed, as I and others gathered in that recording studio in prison to put some of those lyrics to tape. I am sure that recording studio no longer exists at what is now Lompoc Federal Correctional Institution. I am sure of that because good things in prison never last. Here are some of those lyrics:

JUNKIES OF ATTRACTION

They saw each other across the room
Without knowing why
The attraction was immediate
Then both began to sigh

For disappointing heartache
Had been the rule of late
And each was now suspicious
That more might be their fate

That unfounded hope would be their doom
That more was on the way
That person now across the room
Had a price they couldn't pay

Junkies of attraction
The needle rush of love
The anguish of withdrawal
What were you thinking of

Feelings of deep loneliness
The need to find a home
Searching empty handed
No meat and only bone

Your heart is hurt and aching
You can't go on too far
And you wish you'd never started
To wish upon that star

That once seemed oh so promising
The object of your heart
Roses perhaps forever
A couple that'd never part

Junkies of attraction
The needle rush of love
The anguish of withdrawal
What were you thinking of

But you'll never find another
To be what you're to be
An anchor of compassion
On this stormy stormy sea

For only you can give yourself
What you are looking for
The acceptance that you're seeking
That and nothing more

For until you love the whole of you
Your pain and fear and rage
You'll just be seeking others
To put inside your cage

Junkies of attraction
The needle rush of love
The anguish of withdrawal
What were you thinking of

But if you make it lady
Across that stormy sea
I'll be there to meet you
If I, too, am free

Of the binding chains that hold us
To the ancient terror and fear
Of what it might be like
To be so close and near

Junkies of attraction
The needle rush of love
The anguish of withdrawal
What were you thinking of

WAITING IN THE LANES

Did heaven send us here
Thinking there was another
To hold us, to love us
To keep away the pain

Or did heaven set us up
Like pins in a bowling alley
Just like sitting ducks
Waiting in the lanes

Did heaven make it seem
That love was rare and precious
That there was someone special
Waiting for us all

Or did heaven know beforehand
That diamonds weren't forever
That roses always wilted
That passion would always pall

Did heaven put us here
To make it hell for one another
Knowing that a nightmare
Would soon engulf us all

Did heaven know we needed
Someone to remind us
Of fears that needed healing
Of angers in us all

Did heaven send us here
Thinking there was another
To hold us, to love us
To keep away the pain

Or did heaven set us up
Like pins in a bowling alley
Just like sitting ducks
Waiting in the lanes

It seems to me that heaven
Knows that we are trying
To find out what is missing
To find out what is wrong

It seems to me that heaven
Is trying hard to tell us
That each of us to heaven
Really does belong

Did heaven send us here
Thinking there was another
To hold us, to love us
To keep away the pain

Or did heaven set us up
Like pins in a bowling alley
Just like sitting ducks
Waiting in the lanes

LIFEBOATS

You said when you first saw me
You knew you were in love
It was the way I stood there
Looking down from up above

You thought I was Sir Galahad
Come to take you away
Come to make you happy
It was for me that you had prayed

You thought I was a lifeboat
Complete with sail and crew
But the problem was to be
I'd thought the same of you.

When two people are out looking
For another to be whole
They're asking for some trouble
From another troubled soul

For I cannot be for you
What you cannot be for me
The Love that we are seeking
That'll finally set us free

For there's a soul inside us
That's asking for release
And until we do what's asked of us
We'll never be at peace

For time'll go on forever
For what's eternity
But the chance we have today
To set each other free

You thought I was a lifeboat
Complete with sail and crew
But the problem was to be
I'd thought the same of you

DANGER

If bullets don't bother me why do you
With eyes that seem to see
A part inside that I don't know
A part you think is me

I've been places you've read about
Where danger's in the air
Where men packed guns and looked around
To see who else was there

I've flown on planes with contraband
On flights that no one knew
Waited in rooms for phones to ring
Thinking of me and you

If bullets don't bother me why do you
With eyes that seem to see
A part inside that I don't know
A part you think is me

There's danger all around me
In front just like behind
I don't know what you're looking for
But I'm afraid that you will find

That I'm better with guns and danger
Than in a room alone with you
'Cause at least when someone pulls a gun
I know what I should do

If bullets don't bother me why do you
With eyes that seem to see
A part inside that I don't know
A part you think is me

―――――――――

HEY SISTERS

Hey..sisters
Make your move
Your time is coming
Get in your groove

Ever since forever
Or so it does so seem
A life that feels safe to you
Has been but someone's dream

But tomorrow's coming soon
Sooner than you think
So sisters of us all
Push it to the brink

Hey..sisters
Make your move
Your time is coming
Get in your groove

Heaven's poles are changing
Can you feel it in your soul?
Women will be rising
With the changing of their role

Complementary partners
In the universal dance
Everything perfect
Nothing left to chance

Your brothers we are waiting
We're ready for your thing
Anticipatin' wonderin'
What'cha gonna bring

We know you got the power
We know you got the form
We know you got the feelings
And we know you're getting warm

Waitin' deep within you
Is a power that is yours
A power that is feminine
Not his but only hers

That power it is needed
To balance what is male
Then together always moving
We can never ever fail

Hey..sisters
Make your move
Your time is coming
Get in your groove

———————————

We are children of the most high.
That we have forgotten does not make it any less so

———————————

OTHERWISE

Attracted like a homosexual priest to a cute young altar boy, he contemplated the offer before him. She knew he was trapped. He knew it too. It wasn't so much being trapped that bothered him. It was her knowing it.

"How much do you charge?" Her voice was low. It sounded like a good scotch felt. Smooth, but with a burn to it.

"I asked you, how much do you charge?" She repeated the question.

"I heard you the first time."

He looked out over the square. The winter snow had begun to melt. The ground, visible in spots, looked like a wino covered by a thick white blanket; part of it dirty and gray, looking like it needed a washing. It had been years since he had killed a man. It had been years since he had to. Evidently, the years had caught up with him like the past had to the present.

"Where is he?"

"At home."

Her voice was calm, matter of fact. He remembered when he had first heard it. She had laughed and her laugh had been full and natural. He had wondered what kind of woman she was and he had found out. Most people, when you uncovered who they really were, were often different. She had been an exception. She was exactly as he had first thought. He hadn't been wrong but it still didn't mean it was right.

He wondered if she had chosen him beforehand. Knowing exactly what would happen, what would transpire, what would be necessary. Even in the shadows, she looked desirable. Even with the matter at hand, he wanted her.

"What about us?"

At his question, a quiet smile played at the corners of her mouth. The question had not been unexpected. He was sure she had heard it from others before him.

"What about us?" she answered.

"Even if we do get away with it..." His voice trailed off, leaving a question in its wake.

"We will get away with it. I know you can do it." Her voice was certain. Certain as the question it avoided.

There are moments when it appears that choices are made. Choices that lead to unalterable consequences. Choices and moments that, if could be lived again, one would choose otherwise. But that's only the way it appears. It is not certain that those choices, like those moments, were not themselves foreordained, predestined.

She smiled. He liked her smile. When she smiled, it seemed as if the world were right. That promises were kept. That disappointments never happened. That the tooth fairy was on its way. Its arrival imminent.

"Come here."

It was as simple as that. Her words, not a command, not a request, were a bestowal. He stopped not to consider why it was him, not others. It was no longer a matter of price. It was no longer a matter of choice. It was something else altogether.

Later, when all was said and done, he would look back on those moments and consider what would have happened if he had done otherwise and with a laugh he would dismiss such thoughts. For he knew that otherwise had never existed. At least not then.

Woman desired for her desire
Judged for it also
Freed by acceptance

Although HE came forth, it is SHE who sustains the coming.

HE/SHE
Different, yes
But still ONE

RESPECT

I saw two people walking by
It looked like they were in love
And then I had to look again
At what I'd been thinking of

For the two turned out to be men
Holding hands on a public street
My judgments were instant and many my friends
And my thoughts would not retreat

Then I wondered why we couldn't let
Others be as they are
Just what it was in humanity
That won't let us go that far

For all of us are creatures of GOD
No matter what we say
And the life in you is the life in me
For that is nature's way

And as we judge we limit ourselves
By the judgments that we hold
And as far as judging others goes
You know we've all been told

And someday we'll answer to the GOD of us all
About the lines we drew
Between ourselves and the others that GOD
Loved and created too

The rivers run deeper than you and I know
So judgments should not be kept
About the nature of life and love
For we owe all others respect

———————

ZEV COHEN

Jew, a member of a race of Semitic people, an outcast

My father, Zev Cohen, was a Jew among Jews. He died last month after a short illness and with his death a light has gone out in my world. His effect on me was profound and I would like to share with you, Jew and goyim alike, some of who he was.

Gentle and humorous by nature, my father often found himself at odds with other Jews. He would patiently remind me that if Jews were as committed to the truth as they were to fear and guilt there would be no fear in their world. There would only be truth. He would add the same is true, of course, for non-Jews. He was a storyteller in the great tradition, and the tales he would tell would infuriate or enlighten those of us lucky enough to hear them. As an example, my father had a favorite story that drove his brother Alan crazy every time he told it. And he told it every time Alan was around. An avid Zionist, Alan used to say there was nothing wrong with my father's story, it was only what the story implied.

Here is my father's story. I would like to dedicate it to his brother, Alan.

THE PROMISED LAND

It was in the land of Moab where the Jews had wandered for so long it seemed as if they were going around in circles. Now, Moses, because he had talked to God personally, KNEW they were going to the Promised Land. The rest of the tribe of Israel had not heard it from God personally. They had heard it through the grapevine as it were and they weren't all that convinced. It's all in the Bible if you don't believe me, my father used to say. Well, their feet hurt, it was hot, they were always on the go, and it seemed as if it were never going to end. Anyway, there was one woman who had fallen arches and this constant moving about was particularly hard on her.

41

Her name was Rachel and she had no compunctions about making her views known. My father used to say this part is not in the Bible, but if it were, it would fall somewhere between Deuteronomy 10 and Deuteronomy 30, give or take a few verses. Anyway, Rachel was making a big to do about all this wandering, the heat, her feet, and what was supposed to be so good about this so-called Promised Land anyhow. In those days, the idea of heresy was unknown and people were allowed to speak whatever was on their mind. Moses heard about Rachel's kvetching and came over to hear her out. No shrinking violet was our Rachel. She gave it to him all right, the whole nine yards, and I got to hand it to Moses, my father used to say. He didn't slap her across the face and say God was going to punish her for blaspheming and not believing His Word. No, Moses just listened. That's what kind of guy he was. When she had said everything she had to say, Moses took her in his arms, hugged her, patted her consolingly and said, "Rachel, Rachel, don't worry your little head off. When we get there everything's going to be all right." After a long pause, my father would then add, "...and they got there around 3,000 years ago."

Alan would get furious because he said Father's story had anti-Zionist overtones. My father would reply that anyone who thought the problem of the Jews was where they lived had problems to begin with. In his gentle way my father was trying to point out that unless we began to take responsibility for our own problems nothing would ever change for us. It seems, he would say, that as long as Jews can blame others for their situation they are satisfied. This is not to say that others are not guilty of intolerance, hate, bigotry and cruelty; only that until we discover what it is about us that causes life to be the way it seems, will it then change for us. I am sure life loves us, he would say. I think the problem is that we have never ever believed it.

I listened to what my father had to say and I saw the reactions of others. If they knew they were right, they wouldn't get so mad, he would remark and then chuckle. The subject of Gypsies was another one of my father's topics that he and other Jews would go round and round about. They would get furious when he would hypothesize a link between the two peoples. A link he felt was obvious. We are the right arm, they are the left, he would say. The heart, which is in the middle, is what should join us.

The Jews and the Gypsies are the only two peoples, he pointed out, that have wandered homeless all over the earth, outcasts wherever they have gone. The Jews originated in the Middle East, the birthplace of religion in the west; the Gypsies in India, the birthplace of religious thought in the east. We, the Jews, believe we are the chosen people. The Gypsies' stories tell them they are the damned. Our stories merge, however, at the life of Jesus. Everyone knows of our relationship to the matter. The Gypsies, however, have a story that tells of a Gypsy blacksmith, who, knowing nothing of what was going on and needing a few coins, consented to make the nails that crucified the Son of God, a task that all Jewish blacksmiths had previously declined.

"So, so, what does that mean?" My father's friends would yell. My father would reply, "What do you think it means?" He would shake his head sadly, "If we Jews refuse to see the obvious, it is no wonder we so often miss the sublime." Then, he would smile.

My father said that in order for me to solve what it meant for me to be a Jew I would have to seek solutions different from those accepted around me. If those are the solutions, he would say, then we truly are in deep deep trouble.

He died last month in his sleep. Death to him was a paradox. Zen, he told me shortly before his death, I am sure we are not meant to die but I will have to leave that problem for you to solve. Zev Cohen taught me much with his life. And now, because of his death, I would hope that you might learn something of him also. Perhaps, in a small way that will help solve the paradox.

Darryl Robert Schoon

Shalom.

Zen Cohen

We are eternal lights
Passing through temporal darkness
We cannot be harmed
We are love itself

I HAVE SEEN THE DYING LIVE

I have seen the dying live
I have seen the living die
I have heard your unasked questions
As to what and where and why

But I cannot tell you that
Which is not mine to say
For each and every one of you
Must find yourselves this way

The mystery that you live
Is there for you to see
Through subterfuge and pretense
You struggle to be free

From the chains of your own making
From the prisons of your thoughts
That you find yourself now trapped by
You yourself have caught

Sometimes I know it seems
That LOVE is but a lie

That LOVE is but a dream
That only lives to die

But I know it is not so
I know that LOVE is real
But I cannot show it to you
You yourself must heal

I have seen the dying live
I have seen the living die
I have heard your unasked questions
As to what and where and why

But I cannot tell you that
Which is not mine to say
For each and every one one of you
Must find yourselves this way

THE PRINCESS & THE DRAGON
(written for my daughter's eleventh birthday)

Once upon a time, there was a princess. She lived in a castle high above the town. She danced, she laughed, and she had the run of the place (after all, she was the princess).

A few miles away lived a terrible dragon. He lived in a hole. He grumbled, thrashed about, and dreamed of eating the entire town (and all those who inhabited it). And if, in fact, he had known of the princess, he would have wanted to eat her first, for the dragon was not entirely without taste and discrimination.

Luckily for the townsfolk (and the princess), he had a terrible case of dragon's breath. This was why he didn't know of the princess. For his breath was so-ooo bad, everyone knew when he was coming, and they would quickly go on vacation.

One day, as luck (if that's what you call it) would have it, the princess caught a cold. She almost never was sick but this time she couldn't smell a thing (including the dragon)!

That very same day, the dragon had come to town and was thrashing about looking for something (or someone) to eat. The princess had also decided to go to town. She however had gone shopping for some earrings, and was not in the least bit hungry.

The dragon, as terrible as he was (and he was terrible), knew all about his bad breath. His brothers and sisters used to tease him unmercifully about its smell (that's the reason he was living in a hole, not at home with his family), and, as a result, he was very (as you could well imagine) sensitive about it (even for a dragon).

Imagine his surprise (you can do it with your eyes open, if you wish), when he saw the most beautiful creature he had ever seen (the princess, if you haven't figured it out yet) walking downtown looking in the windows. She, looking at a particular set of earrings, did not even notice him (when she was shopping, nothing could distract her attention—not even a dragon).

It was the most beautiful set of earrings she had ever seen. They were long and shimmering and studded with diammels. She went to the entrance to try the door. It, however, was locked as the shopkeepers had fled at the first whiff of his (the dragon's) breath. She rattled the door and knocked to no avail. Vexed (princesses are known to be so sometimes), she went back to look in the window.

The terrible dragon, trying to intimidate the princess, let loose a flame of fire aiming twenty feet from where she stood. As fate would have it, the flames melted away the heavy locks on the door, and it (the door) immediately opened wide. The princess knew a miracle when she saw one (after all, she was a princess and could tell a miracle from a common everyday occurrence such as a flat tire).

She turned around so she could see the "cause" of this miraculous event (She knew, of course, that God really caused all miracles, but that they are brought about in many different ways—in this case, by a dragon). Being well mannered and spiritually aware, she smiled at the dragon, gave him a light curtsy (he was, after all, still only a dragon), and hurried inside to try on the earrings. Looking at herself in the mirror, she thought they were as beautiful as she had first imagined. She signed her name to a receipt, and on it noted the price and item (being the princess, she had an unlimited amount of credit—this fact greatly facilitating her many shopping sprees in town).

When she left, the dragon was waiting right in front of the door. For when she had smiled and curtseyed at him (he, after all, was only a dragon), he had been immediately smitten with love (love in the higher, not romantic, sense of the word). Her simple act of thanks had been, for him, a miracle (a miracle being any act that transforms and releases—love being the most common method).

And because of her kindness, he (the dragon) had the biggest smile on his face that could fit comfortably on the face of a dragon (this smile, in fact, was a little too big but he was so-ooo happy he didn't even notice the slight discomfort it caused).

Now, no one had ever seen a dragon smile. The princess, however, thought it normal for everyone smiled wherever she went (smiles, it should be noted, are an order of miracles, themselves, and are oftentimes the "cause" of wonderful events, and this time was to be no exception to the general rule).

When he smiled, the princess saw in the back of his mouth (behind the last tooth on the left), a huge pot of old cheese. She immediately bade the dragon to follow her to the city dump (by this time, he would have followed her wherever she asked). She then had him tilt his head just so (and when she demonstrated this for him it made him love her even more), and the huge pot of cheese was immediately dislodged and fell straight out of his mouth.

If you, the readers, haven't yet figured it out, the pot of cheese was the "cause" of his (the dragon's) bad breath, put there years before by his brothers and sisters while he slept (this was a common form of trickery that young dragons play on one another).

Thus, the young dragon was cured of a bad case of dragon's breath by the beautiful young princess. She (the princess) went back to her castle to show her earrings to her friends, and he (the dragon) went home to get even with his brothers and sisters.

Will a future that never happens decide what we do today
Will a past that ever lingers be the reason we feel this way

WOUNDED EAGLE

I can see your pretty colors
I can hear the whirring of your wings
And as I watch your flight around me
Ancient feelings do you bring

But you'd better keep your distance
Though you're right 'bout what you see
I'm an eagle but I'm wounded
And I'm searching for a key

Don't disturb a wounded animal
Though you hear his wounded cry
Till he's healed he is dangerous
I'm an eagle and can't fly

It seems at times I need you
So I can fly and soar again
High above the mountains
Like I used to do once when

I was an eagle proud and free
And my flight was clear and strong

But I haven't flown in many moons
And now this is my song

Don't disturb a wounded animal
Though you hear his wounded cry
Till he's healed he is dangerous
I'm an eagle and can't fly

But there is something 'bout you
That tells me deep inside
I need you for my healing
But it runs against my pride

To be wounded and still want you
To want to soar the skies with you
When I cannot fly except in dreams
And I don't know what to do

Don't disturb a wounded animal
Though you hear his wounded cry
Till he's healed he is dangerous
I'm an eagle and can't fly

FRIENDSHIP, MARSHALL, LAW SCHOOL, AND THE MOVIE BUSINESS

In my life there are friends who have over the years played important and critical roles in what has transpired. Marshall Thurber is one such friend. We met at Hastings Law School in San Francisco in 1966. He was from Vermont and, at the time, eager to take on the world. I, already having been through much of the political and social chaos of the 1960s, was much more distrustful of the world and much less inclined to get involved.

But with his optimistic energy, Marshall managed to convince me to write a piece for the Hastings Law School newspaper, which he had

49

been chosen to edit. A freshman editor of the December edition was a tradition at Hastings because the second and third year students were all studying hard for their mid-year exams. But what was to happen to that December edition was not to be in the Hastings tradition.

Marshall assembled a December issue quite unlike any that had preceded it. Usually, the Hastings newspaper was an embarrassment to journalism and social involvement, a testament to the bland neutrality of a profession that chooses its side based on who is paying. This issue was different. So different Marshall would be threatened with expulsion and forced to retain a lawyer.

Marshall chose my piece for the lead article. The headline of the law school newspaper boldly stated "THE CHURCH RESPONSIBLE FOR ACTS OF GOD." This refers to a fundamental tenet of tort law that holds no one legally liable for what are termed acts of God, e.g. hurricanes, floods, earthquakes, and other natural disasters. I argued in the article that God, being just, would never shirk his responsibilities and therefore an answer must exist. I posited that since there are those among us who claim to be his agents here on earth and are recognized as such by their tax-free status, they must be the ones God intended to take care of His earthly liabilities.

This and other articles (e.g., on the Vietnam War) Marshall had assembled caused the Dean of the Hastings Law School to threaten to expel Marshall and close down the student council and the newspaper if the newspaper went out to the alumni. Marshall felt strongly this was a first amendment free speech issue. I felt that since this was the United States, when push came to shove, constitutional issues really didn't count for much. In the end, the student council gave in to the Dean's edict, the newspaper was not issued, and Marshall was left with passing out informational leaflets to a group of future lawyers most of whom could not care less.

My friendship with Marshall continued through the years and it was natural I would inform Marshall in 1981 when I had decided to write screenplays. Marshall told me he would introduce me to Michael Shultz, someone in the movie business who had attended some of

Marshall's business seminars. My meeting with Michael was very low key and we agreed to keep in touch through Marshall.

Shortly thereafter, at one of Marshall's seminars I suddenly had an idea for a movie, an idea I told to Michael's wife, Gloria, who was also at the seminar and said Michael would love it. My idea was for a movie to be called "La Vacance / The Vacation", a story about a suburban couple (Chevy Chase and Jill Clayburg) who are supposed to take a long delayed honeymoon to Paris when the husband, secretly wanting a new Corvette, instead pressures the family into a vacation in Mexico, during which the grandmother dies and is put up on the roof of the family station wagon, which is then subsequently stolen, to wit, a guilt driven black comedy.

We flew down to Los Angeles to meet Michael and to celebrate my daughter's sixth birthday which she requested to spend at L'Ermitage, a hotel in Beverly Hills where we had previously stayed. The limo driver from the hotel asked what we were doing in L.A., and when told, informed us that he knew of Michael Shultz, that Michael was, in fact, a director best known for his movie, Car Wash.

That evening Michael taped my telling of the plot, and he and Gloria and their two children celebrated my daughter's birthday with us, the cake happily ordered by the limo driver. Two weeks later, Michael called me to say that he had spoken to Carl Reiner who liked the idea and might help in writing the screenplay. Then, a month later Michael asked for permission to submit the idea to Universal and Lorimar for possible production. I, of course, gave my permission. Then, nothing happened. At least nothing until my children returned from the local movie theater months later saying they had just seen my movie, "National Lampoon's Vacation", with Chevy Chase.

Michael denied any connection between my idea and "National Lampoon's Vacation"; and although nothing could be done, it was not an experience that would sit well with me. But within a few years it would be soon overshadowed when I was arrested for conspiracy to possess and sell cocaine in a government sting operation designed to nab a Colombian drug dealer.

Marshall again was to play a key role. Almost at the same time I was arrested, he had purchased a gold mine in Nevada with Jac Holzman. Holzman was something of a legend in Hollywood. He had started Elektra Records and later bought Panavision and was a technical advisor to Warner Brothers. I was to spend the next eight months at Marshall and Jac's gold mine in Hawthorne, NV, waiting for the resolution of my case, and the I Ching made it clear, proximity notwithstanding, Hollywood would still remain out of my reach.

As my prison sentence drew to a close, I remembered more than ever what had happened with my movie idea and the movie, "National Lampoon's Vacation". My life would have been far different if things had been otherwise. Ironically, Marshall had unexpectedly encountered Michael who had again denied knowing of any connection between my idea and the movie that was produced. But even if there was a connection, I would eventually understand that things had truly turned out for the best, that I had gained far more by going to prison than I ever would have by going to Hollywood.

My ten year prison sentence not only gave me the incentive to meditate, it gave me the time to write. And, in the last year of my sentence, screenplays replaced the fiction, lyrics, and verse that preceded them. Eleven screenplays were written in the last twelve months. Prison had provided me with an unintended sabbatical, a writer's dream, to have enough time to write. I certainly had the time.

I now know prison gave me something else Hollywood with its promises could never give. Prison allowed me to let go in a way I never could on my own. It was in prison where personal control is impossible that I learned that it is not even needed. I learned in prison that we are truly in God's hands, and that all we have to do is to "let go and let God" as the trite saying truthfully says. And, the fact that I had to be forced to let go in order to let God, is testimony only to my own stubbornness and His mysterious ways.

December 17, 1990, a tramp freighter lies idle in San Pedro Harbor. Black, rusted, and low in the water, it has been there for the past two weeks, rumored to have been confiscated by the Coast Guard and the DEA. Just off of Terminal Island, it is in plain view of the Terminal Island Federal Penitentiary where I and other convicts watch it each and every day. At anchor, moved only by the tides, it reeks of contraband and romance, of rusted hopes and of faraway ports, of movies in black and white, and of Bogie and Bacall. That's when I thought of...

RIO DE LAS CUERDAS / RIVER OF THE STRINGS

EXT. NEW YORK CITY – DAY

A beat up delivery van, on its sides the words "ALAN's 110% KOSHER FRANKS," is caught in a traffic jam in midtown Manhattan on a spring day. The traffic light turns green and the cars barely inch forward.

INT. VAN - DAY

WOODY ALLEN, in an "Alan's 110% Kosher Franks" T-shirt and Levi's is driving. In the passenger seat doing her nails is MADONNA dressed in a secondhand 1930s-style dress, fish net stockings, her hair in Marcel waves. Woody Allen is in the midst of a conversation more frustrating than the traffic.

> WOODY ALLEN
> I really don't think you should change
> your name. Emily McDonough is nice
> enough. Marlene Madonna doesn't
> even sound real. You know my analyst
> says that unless we accept who we
> think we are, we'll never find out who
> we really are.

> MADONNA
> (concentrating on her nails)

Do you believe in reincarnation, Alan?

> WOODY ALLEN
> (ignoring her question)
> I'd never change my name. Alan Woodstein is good enough for me just as Emily McDonough should be good enough for you. Where did you ever come up with a name like Marlene Madonna?

She puts her nails out the window to dry.

> MADONNA
> I think I might be Marlene Dietrich reincarnated.

The engine dies when she says this. Woody Allen restarts it. This is not his day.

> WOODY ALLEN
> We were making progress, Emily. I sent your songs to three record companies and they all said you had promise. But now you just want to do Marlene Dietrich impersonations. What's wrong with still doing your own stuff?

Her hands still out the window, Madonna shakes them to hasten her nails drying.

> MADONNA
> I believe that we should only express our true selves. If you don't want to be my agent any more then just say so, Alan. I'll just have to find someone else.

WOODY ALLEN
Three record companies said they
liked your songs and I thought we
wouldn't have to sleep in my van any
more.
(shakes his head in disbelief)

And where do you think we're going
to get the money to produce your
Marlene Dietrich musical? It's not
going to be cheap. I can see it costing
eight hundred thousand dollars
minimum.

MADONNA
That's your job.

Madonna reaches over and pats Woody Allen reassuringly on his
shoulder, making sure at the same time she doesn't mess up her
nails.

MADONNA
You need to have more faith, Alan.

WOODY ALLEN
No, Emily. We need to have more
money.

EXT. NEW YORK CITY - DAY

High POV. Montage of New York City scenes as a particularly
soulful rendition of George Gershwin's SUMMERTIME plays in the
background on a clarinet. The shot ends on Woody Allen playing his
clarinet in front of a fast food restaurant. Onlookers and passersby
toss coins into his open clarinet case on which a sign is taped,
reading:

CLOSE UP: HELP PRODUCE A PLAY

INT. FAST FOOD RESTAURANT - EARLY EVENING

Woody Allen waits at the checkout counter, his tray piled high with his and Madonna's order. He pays with quarters, dimes, and nickels as those behind him impatiently wait for him to finish. He takes the tray over to Madonna who is seated at a table.

> MADONNA
> Lots of food tonight, Alan.

> WOODY ALLEN
> Money will get you whatever you
> want.

They dive hungrily into their food.

> MADONNA
> Did you find out how much they want
> for that theater?

> WOODY ALLEN
> Yes.

> MADONNA
> How much?

> WOODY ALLEN
> They're asking $15,000 per week and
> one month's deposit up front.

> MADONNA
> That's not too much.

> WOODY ALLEN
> That's because you don't have to get
> the money.

> MADONNA
>
> If I can do Marlene Dietrich, you can
> raise the money.

> WOODY ALLEN
>
> How?

> MADONNA
>
> I don't know, but I know you can. You
> see, Alan, even if you don't have faith
> in yourself, I do. Somehow, you'll get
> it. That's why you're my agent.

Madonna rises from the table, leans over, and kisses Woody Allen
on his forehead.

> MADONNA
>
> I'm going to the bathroom. You just sit
> here and think about it. I know you'll
> come up with something.

She leaves. Woody Allen, looking dejected and worried, sees a
newspaper left on another table. He picks it up and begins to read.
An article catches his attention. The headlines read:

CLOSE UP: MILLIONS OF DOLLARS IN DRUG TRADE

> WOODY ALLEN'S VOICE
>
> (VO as Woody reads the article)
> Despite government efforts, the U.S.
> drug trade grows larger and larger. In
> clubs and bars, big money is
> exchanged every night for America's
> party drug of choice. Called by
> different names - snort, toot, coke, the
> white lady, whatever you want to call
> it – it's cocaine hydrochloride.

Woody Allen reads and rereads the article. He is mesmerized by its implications. He carefully tears it out of the newspaper, folds it and puts it in his pocket before Madonna returns.

> MADONNA
> Ready to go?

> WOODY ALLEN
> All ready.

> MADONNA
> Think of anything?

> WOODY ALLEN
> I've got some ideas.

> MADONNA
> I knew you would. Come on.

She takes his arm and they exit the restaurant.

EXT. NEW YORK STREETS - NIGHT

The van seems to be going in no particular direction when Woody Allen spots a parking place in a business and residential neighborhood and pulls in.

INT. VAN - NIGHT

Woody Allen and Madonna move to the rear of the van where a mattress covers the floor. While Madonna gets a nightie out of her suitcase, Woody Allen retrieves a sleeping bag and returns to the driver's seat. Looking into the rear view mirror, he tries to catch a glimpse of Madonna's partially-clad body as she readies herself for bed. Finally, under the covers, she smiles at him in the mirror and blows a kiss. Woody is in the sleeping bag sitting in the driver's seat.

> MADONNA
> Goodnight, Alan.

WOODY ALLEN
Goodnight, Emily.

Wrapped in his sleeping bag, Woody Allen pensively stares at the roof of the van. After a while he retrieves the newspaper article and in the light of the street lamp slowly reads it again. Putting it away, and after making sure Madonna is fast asleep, he quietly begins to dress.

INT. CAR - NIGHT

A government-issue black-sidewalled car is coming up a street. Inside are TWO MEN, WESTON and TOM. Tom is driving while Weston is trying to decipher the static coming in on his walkie-talkie.

WESTON
(into his walkie-talkie)
Please repeat. This is Alpha Unit.
Please repeat.

Weston holds the unit close to his ear as he tries to make out what is being said.

WESTON
Alpha Unit receives you. Ten Four.
Will   terminate   surveillance   as
requested. Over and out.

TOM
Quitting time, Weston?

WESTON
Done for the day.

Weston picks up a clipboard and logs the time. At the top of the sheet of paper in bold large letters are the words:

CLOSE UP: U.S. DEPARTMENT OF JUSTICE DRUG
ENFORCEMENT AGENCY

> WESTON
> I don't know about you, Tom, but I
> could sure use a drink.

> TOM
> Where to?

> WESTON
> The first bar you find.

Tom sees a bar, slows down passing Woody's parked van, and parks.
He and Weston walk back past Woody's van and enter the bar.

INT. BAR - NIGHT

It's a crowded and noisy yuppie-type bar. Tom and Weston make
their way over to the counter where the BARTENDER comes over
to take their order.

> BARTENDER
> What'll it be?

> TOM
> A vodka tonic.

> WESTON
> Same for me.

The drinks are delivered and Tom pays.

> TOM
> This round's on me.

> WESTON
> Thanks.

                    TOM
        Cheers.

They drink up. Now, relaxed, they survey the crowded room. As
they look, a telephoto shot picks up Woody Allen as he enters the
bar. Nervously, he looks around and begins to make his way in their
direction.

                    TOM
                (sipping his drink)
        Why do people use drugs? They can
        kill themselves just as easily with
        booze.

                  WESTON
        It's probably the excitement of doing
        something illegal.

                    TOM
        Wonder what would happen if they
        legalized drugs?

                  WESTON
                (laughing)
        We'd be out of a job.

                    TOM
        Think it'll happen?

                  WESTON
        Not anytime soon. Don't worry, Tom.
        We can ride this one till we retire.

Weston finishes his drink and motions the bartender for a refill for
the both of them. Woody Allen is now at the bar, next to the two
men

                  WESTON
        Two more vodka tonics

The bartender sees Woody Allen.

> BARTENDER
> (to Woody Allen)
> What'll it be?

> WOODY ALLEN
> Do you have mineral water?

> BARTENDER
> I've got tonic water.

> WOODY ALLEN
> One tonic water, please.

Weston, sipping his drink, watches curiously.

> WESTON
> (to Woody Allen)
> Just saying no to alcohol, tobacco, and
> drugs?

> WOODY ALLEN
> Actually, no. It's just no to alcohol and
> tobacco. It's yes to drugs.

Tom, hearing Woody's comment and nudged by Weston's elbow, turns to listen in on the conversation.

> WESTON
> (in a friendly and interested manner)
> So it's yes to using drugs?

> WOODY ALLEN
> (feeling more confident)
> Not for me. I don't use them. I sell
> them.

Tom and Weston are now completely focused in on Woody Allen.

> WESTON
> (incredulously, yet as one who can be trusted)
> How interesting. What do you sell?

> WOODY ALLEN
> (smugly, lowering his voice)
> Snort, toot, coke, the white lady, whatever you want to call it—it's cocaine hydrochloride.

> WESTON
> (smiling)
> Well, well, well, what a stroke of luck! You may be just what we're looking for.

Weston extends his hand to Woody, who shakes it

> WESTON
> (motioning towards Tom)
> This is my partner Bill, and my name is Joe.

> WOODY ALLEN
> Pleased to meet you. My name is Alan, Alan Woodstein.

Tom and Woody now shake hands.

> TOM
> Is Woodstein Wood-s-t-e-i-n or Wood-s-t-i-e-n?

> WOODY ALLEN
> S-t-e-i-n. Woodstein.

TOM
Thanks.

WOODY ALLEN
No problem. It's nice that you're interested. Usually people don't care about things like that.

WESTON
Well, Bill and I are different than most people, Alan.

Pointing to Woody's empty glass.

WESTON
Another one?

WOODY ALLEN
Why yes. That would be nice. Thank you.

WESTON
(to the bartender)
Another round for the three of us, please.

WESTON
(lowering his voice, conspiratorially)
Frankly, Alan, Bill and I are buyers of what you sell and we're looking for another source. Our old supplier can't seem to deliver all the coke we can sell.

WOODY ALLEN
(confidently sipping his tonic water)
Whatever you need I can get.

                    TOM
Whatever?

                WOODY ALLEN
That's right. Whatever.

                    WESTON
Listen Al, I mean Alan, is there a
number at which we can phone
you?...a pager number or cell phone?

                WOODY ALLEN
No.

                    WESTON
No number at all?

                WOODY ALLEN
No, no number at all.

                    TOM
I like your style, Alan. Real discreet.
No phones. No pager. That's real
professional. How about meeting Joe
and me tomorrow to discuss business?
Here at eight tomorrow night?

                WOODY ALLEN
Eight p.m. would be fine.

They shake hands.

                WOODY ALLEN
Thanks for the tonic water. I'll see you
guys tomorrow.

Woody Allen leaves. At the door he turns and waves goodbye. Tom
and Weston wave back.

EXT. NEW YORK STREET - NIGHT

Outside the bar, Woody Allen breaks into a spontaneous dance of happiness. His face is one big grin. He skips down the street to the van where he quietly unlocks the door and gets in. He sits and savors his accomplishment then starts to get into his sleeping bag. He then stops and tip toes back to where Madonna sleeps. He kneels beside her and gently kisses her on the cheek

> WOODY ALLEN
> (whispering)
> We're going to be rich, Emily. We're
> going to get the money for the theater.

In her sleep, Madonna smiles.

> This morning I remembered
> The Father's love
> The Mother's compassion
> Wake up someone called out to me
> I am was my answer
> It is you who are still asleep

> We need do nothing, for our Father loves to give
> He waits upon only our readiness to receive

THE DRAGON'S HOUR

> Confucius Mao Deng Xiao-Ping
> It all adds up to the same damn thing

Chinese people afraid to speak
Beaten down oh so meek

3000 years of history
3000 years of tyranny
Until the dragon rises up
China will remain corrupt

Tienanmen ain't nothing new
Thousands die, one man rules
Silken gowns, blind man's stitch
Life has always been a bitch

Yin and Yang so long ago
The Chinese knew the truth was so
Yin and Yang each a pole
Each a part of a greater whole

But China chose to reject Yin
Emotion, feeling, the feminine
Its culture froze, invention ceased
Mother Nature wasn't pleased

Confucius said the way to be
Was to act appropriately
Follow rules, not your heart
Deny your feelings, act your part

Now 3000 years have passed
China's glory did not last
China died a death within
Without feelings, without Yin

But inside of China's soul
Lives a dragon without a role
Waiting for the people's call
Waiting for their tears to fall

Calling forth the power of Yin
Calling up what's always been
The source of China's greatest power
For what will be the dragon's hour

When free I discovered my limits
When imprisoned I found there were none
Had the wheel not turned I would have been
stuck with limitations
Turn, turn, oh wheel, turn, turn

B UNIT COT ROOM

Terminal Island Federal Penitentiary, unlike Lompoc Federal Prison Camp, looked like a prison. It had gun towers with armed guards and many on the yard had tattoos and extremely long sentences. But the hacks didn't hassle the inmates like they did at Lompoc Camp. At Lompoc Camp, the inmates only had a short time to go and weren't about to jeopardize their release dates by standing up for themselves. At Terminal Island, inmates were doing twenty years to life and the attitude of the hacks showed it. Having longer sentences and less to lose, many of the inmates at Terminal Island might just decide to kill you if they were needlessly hassled. And because of that, the hacks at Terminal Island left the inmates alone to do their time, making time much easier to do.

The cot room in B Unit was where inmates new to the unit were first assigned. Previously a recreation room, it had been converted into an open dorm as a result of the exploding prison population caused by the draconian sentences being handed down. It was noisy, chaotic, crowded; and most inmates couldn't wait to get out of the cot room and into one of the smaller, quieter four man cubes. I, however, liked the cot room and stayed there far longer than anyone expected.

Most of those in the cot room were brothers straight from the ghetto, and many had sentences longer than their current age. These were black kids that white society had judged as criminally dangerous and wanted off the streets forever. But living in the cot room showed me another more fundamental truth. These were kids who had never had a chance except the chances they took.

One day a white boy was transferred into the cot room and the longer he was there, the more everyone wanted him to leave. He talked endlessly and needlessly. And it became apparent that much of what he said wasn't true. In short, he was someone no one wanted to do time with. But much to our collective disappointment, it began to dawn on us that he liked the cot room and wasn't anxious to leave.

The tension in the room began to mount. The mood changed noticeably when he entered and when he left. He, however, didn't seem to notice; and if he did notice, he didn't seem to care. But in prison, as in life, things often come to a head and it was obvious that was where things were headed.

I played no part in what was to happen. I took no part in its planning. I can only testify as to what I witnessed. It was the white boy's bathing habits or rather lack of them that was to bring about the inevitable confrontation. Since he washed his sheets rarely and himself even less, the smell in that overcrowded cot room soon become unbearable. The brothers determined something had to be done.

I watched as they planned the confrontation. It was agreed it would take place during the four o'clock count when everyone would be present. And after the hacks had made their rounds, it began. One by one, they spoke, telling him what was wrong and what they wanted him to do. Some put laundry soap, toothpaste and other supplies on his bed. And one of the brothers told him, "You don't have to talk to nobody who don't want to listen. You can always talk to me. You know I'll listen to anything." The confrontation turned out to be a lesson in humanity everyone could afford to learn.

The cot room was different after that. The white boy washed his sheets regularly and his personal hygiene changed for the better. What didn't change, however, was what had caused the cot room to become so overcrowded in the first place. It's obvious that most of the brothers' crimes were the result of economic conditions in the United States, conditions that haven't changed and conditions that are as criminal as the behavior they cause, conditions that have benefited the few with so much and have punished the many with so little.

———————

The brothers are down
locked up and slammed
by the cold motherfuckers
who rule this land
who say they care
'bout liberty
but you know it hurts 'em
if a brother goes free
what chance they got
these brothers from town
in a world so cold
it puts them down
for who they are
and look and feel
but deep inside
they know they're real
but where's this got 'em
in a world so cold
they now got attitudes
raw and bold
where they're actin' tough
being gangster dudes
rough and ready
and mean and rude and
carryin' guns and
feelin' no fear

intimidating pressing
beyond their years
they know the streets
not books and schools
they know for them
there ain't no rules
cause the cold motherfuckers
who run the game
are gonna make sure
they take the blame
for all that's wrong
in society
the new fall guys
they won't let free
'cause the cold motherfuckers
are doing their best
to jail 'em up
and kill the rest
but the brothers are real
they got love and heart
and I'm waiting for them
to play their part
in God's great plan
for this world of ours
when we'll all be free
of prisons and bars
but now ain't then
and the times are bad
and the brothers you know
are being had
cause life on the streets
is suicide
and going that way
is one hard ride
so I'm watchin' it all
like a TV show
and I tell myself
I'd like to know
that it's gonna turn out

so the brothers'll be
moving and popping
and finally free
but the cold motherfuckers
have lots of power
and it may not be
the brothers' hour
so I sit here on
my prison bed
and hope the brothers
can keep their heads
and make it through
these hard ass days
cause the cold motherfuckers
have got their ways

(Austin Songwriters Contest, lyrics, 2005 1st Place)

———————

Every time the house lights dim
We think the end has come
With each and every curtain's rise
We believe it's just begun

The eyes we use to see with
Are useless with the Light
They show us only shadows
And creatures in the night

With minds so shut so tightly
It's a wonder we'll ever see
That we're who we seek already
And that will always be

———————

Doubt, a small light in the sea of darkness, has no value in the ocean of Light.

―――――――

A TALE OF TWO CITIES

It was the best of times and the worst of times. And whether it was one or the other could depend on who you were and what city you lived in.

In the city of Oakland, California, a man borrowed his girlfriend's car. He was black as was she. Later that day, the man was arrested after having bought a small amount of rock cocaine in one of Oakland's poorer black neighborhoods. The police not only arrested the man, they seized his girlfriend's car as well, citing a newly enacted law giving the state the right to seize any asset which had been used in the commission of a drug related crime.

The black woman sued the state to get her car back. Her lawyers pointed out that the woman was not responsible for the actions of her boyfriend, that it was her car, and there was no evidence that she had prior knowledge of his intention to buy drugs. The state answered that the black woman's prior knowledge of the crime was irrelevant. That current law allowed them to seize any and all assets committed in the commission of drug related crimes and that her car was now theirs to sell.

The case made its way all the way up to the United States Supreme Court. There, the Justices in their finite wisdom held that the state did have the right to summarily seize her car. The court ruled in essence that the societal issues at stake, i.e. the right of the state to protect itself against the proliferation of the illegal sale of drugs, were such that the property rights of the woman were subrogated to the right of the state to "protect" itself.

Later, in the city of New York, it was determined that Raoul Salinas, the brother of the President of Mexico, had used Citicorp Bank to wash hundred of millions of dollars in illegal drug profits prior to depositing them into secret Swiss bank accounts. The President of Mexico, Mr. Salinas' brother, Harvard educated Carlos Salinas, shortly after leaving the presidency, himself fled to Ireland, a country which has no extradition treaty with Mexico.

Mexico, which has drawn the wrath of U.S. politicians for not aggressively supporting the U.S. driven worldwide war on drugs, arrested Raoul Salinas for murder and for his drug related crimes. And, as a result of the investigation into Raoul Salinas' crimes, it was also discovered that Citicorp Bank had assisted Mr. Salinas by failing to notify the U. S. government of the huge amounts of unreported cash being deposited in its bank prior to being wired to banks in Switzerland; this lack of notification being a significant violation of U.S. law.

The issue of whether or not the officers of Citicorp or its owners had prior knowledge of Citicorp's crime in assisting Raoul Salinas in laundering hundreds of millions of dollars is moot. Their prior knowledge is irrelevant because nothing was ever done by the U.S. government to pursue Citicorp, the richest bank in New York, for its gross violations of U.S. law.

Unlike the car owned by the poor black woman in Oakland, California, the wealthiest bank in New York City was never seized as an asset for its role in a drug related crime, nor were any of its officers charged. It was the best of times and the worst of times. And whether it was one or the other could depend on who you were and what city you lived in.

Hey, Mr. Bennett
Still hooked on nicotine
You ain't no fuckin' drug czar
You're just a cheap dope fiend

Once we had a drug czar
To make America strong
To fight a war against all drugs
'Cause America says they're wrong

So the President himself
Of these United States
Picked a man who said he would
Clean up degenerates

The man was William Bennett
A teacher at some school
The man seemed so outspoken
That he seemed to me a fool

His solutions were quite simple
But I knew they wouldn't work
'Cause underneath his Ph.D.
The guy was just a jerk

Hey Mr. Bennett
Still hooked on nicotine
You ain't no fuckin drug czar
You're just a cheap dope fiend

Well Mr. Bennett promised
In a speech that he would set
An example for Americans
So everyone could get

A sense of his commitment
To fight this newest war
Against the threat that's knocking
On America's front door

He said he'd give up cigarettes
A couple of packs a day
So Americans would realize
The truth in what he'd say

But Bennett couldn't do it
He couldn't make it clean
He found he was a junkie
Strung out on nicotine

Hey Mr. Bennett
Still hooked on nicotine
You ain't no fuckin drug czar
You're just a cheap dope fiend

Bennett then decided
Because of politics
To appear that he had triumphed
That his habit he had kicked

So he found a chewing gum
Chock full of nicotine
That allowed him to look
Like a real Mr. Clean

But it's quite the common knowledge
That addicts often lie
Especially politicians
Who are in the public eye

So everytime he needed
A nicotine run
He would reach for a stick
Of nicotine gum

Hey Mr. Bennett
Still hooked on nicotine
You ain't no fuckin' drug czar
You're just a cheap dope fiend

Well America has got
What America deserves
Two-faced politicians
Full of lies and full of nerve

For people want to think
That simple answers work
So they listen to the words
Of any stupid jerk

Who will tell them the lies
That they really want to hear
And politicians breed
In these pools of people's fears

For Bennett is no different
Than all the maggots born
In the stinking rotten garbage
Of our legislative porn

Hey Mr. Bennett
Still hooked on nicotine
You ain't no fuckin' drug czar
You're just a cheap dope fiend

———————

To hear my heart's song, I need only listen

———————

With curiosity instead of caution
I rest in the protection of Self.

———————

THE HELLS ANGELS PARTY

The criminalization of America in the 1980s resulted in an explosion
of the prison population. And whereas taxpayers have seen its effects
mainly in the demands of its tax collectors, we saw it in our

immediate living conditions. So many more were being sentenced and the sentences were so much longer, the need for more higher security prisons forced the U.S. Bureau of Prisons to convert most of their low-level security prisons into higher-level institutions in order to accommodate the increased criminalization of America.

As a result, Lompoc Federal Prison Camp, like so many others, underwent a radical change. A barbed wire fence was erected around its perimeter in order to accommodate the soon-to-arrive influx of higher security level inmates. And the problem for the U.S. Bureau of Prisons became what to do with all the low security inmates when their low security facilities had become transformed into higher security institutions.

As the transition inevitably came closer, more and more of the camp's inmates were transferred out to other camps or other prisons. And that was the reason the Hells Angels threw a going away party at Lompoc Prison Camp right before the rest of us were to be sent to destinations yet unknown.

Since a great many Americans are still personally unfamiliar with what prison is like (although increasingly more and more are now finding out), it is important to understand that race and other socioeconomic factors become very important in jail. It seems to be an almost reflexive reaction that when one is cast into unfamiliar surroundings, one gravitates to what appears familiar, race being the most obvious and visible factor. That being said, I, being Chinese by birth, was still invited to the party thrown by the Hells Angels just prior to the Camp being closed down.

My previous exposure to the Hells Angels had been in the early days of the Haight-Ashbury when they were a part of that inexplicably inclusive coming together of outcasts in America. As lines became drawn, however, the Angels and the hippies grew apart; the problems at Altamont exposing a mutual misunderstanding in a previously hoped-for acid dream.

Although I had been invited, I still was a bit leery of attending. Not that I would be in any danger, but I personally only knew a few of the Angels and as I stated before, familiarity is an important consideration in the slammer. Instead, I decided to take a nap, which, if any of you who haven't yet done time someday do so, you will find to be a wonderful way of working off your sentence.

A knock on my door woke me up. It was one of the Angels motioning me to get up, reminding me that a party to which I had been invited was in progress. I walked down the hallway to where the festivities were taking place. It was in a room now filled with people. Guys were sitting tightly packed together on upper and lower bunks, and a table was covered with food. What I remember is the large amount of canned chicken. The cans were available in the commissary and weren't cheap. Either the Angels had kicked down big time for this party or they had ripped off the commissary. Either way, it was a generous gesture.

I had obviously come in the middle of their party, just when another activity was about to begin. Most of the attendees seemed to be waiting and after I finished off as much of the chicken as was polite, I leaned back against the wall and waited for what was next. The conversation grew quieter and somebody asked for the overhead light to be turned off. And, with the proper mood now set, someone next to the table lamp began to read aloud.

The hoots and hollers made it obvious that this reading was not a first time event. Most of those present were familiar with the book and there were numerous cries to recount what had happened previously to the heroine. Her name was Debbie and the title of the book, I believe, was "Debbie and Her Dog."

In some circles, stories of sex between dogs and girls, and girls and girls and boys and girls might not be acceptable. This crowd of Hells Angels and friends, however, was more broadminded. Not only did the numerous and varied sexual encounters hold their interest, but the story line as well seemed to be appreciated. I was amazed and heartened. It was obvious from what was happening that schools could interest far more students in reading if they only tried a different approach.

I am not suggesting that "Jane and Spot" be replaced by "Debbie and Her Dog." But, if the truth be known, to many of the Hells Angels and others in prison, school was not much different from where they now found themselves. Schools don't teach students to think. Instead they tell them what to think and what to do. Hells Angels, more than most, don't respond well to coercion even when it's called education. And, that's the part of the Hells Angels I easily understood.

IF YOU CAN LOVE A CAT
WHY CAN'T YOU LOVE A DOG LIKE ME

A leash won't stay around my neck
A collar don't feel right
I ain't some poodle to be shown
Around the town at night

I can't play dead sit up and beg
Do tricks like some dogs can
Won't roll over like a dog named Rover
Guess I'm too much like a man

If you can love a cat
Why can't you love a dog like me

I know you like me honey
Cause I know I make you itch
And it makes you hot and bothered
When you see me with a bitch

But you know I'm just a dog
Who likes to cat around
So won't you love me honey
When I'm in your part of town

I ain't pretending baby
To be some pedigree

You know I eat 'bout anything
These dog eyes still can see

But I know you'll love it baby
If you let me in your yard
Cause I can see it in your eyes
You like it good and hard

If you can love a cat
Why can't you love a dog like me

So if you find you're in the mood
To have some low down fun
To play with balls fetch a bone
To see how well I run

Just whistle honey real low
A sound that I can hear
And put on something real nice
Something short and sheer

'Cause when I see you looking like
A dream I've always had
It turns this cat into a dog
That wants you real bad

If you can love a cat
Why can't you love a dog like me

Ancient doors
And dungeons open
Light floods in
GOD it feels good

Relationships are like bridges. They carry you from where you think
you need something from others to where you know there is nothing
you do not already have.

ASSIGNED SEATING II

Willie Horton, the poster boy of Reagan's presidency, pretty much
did in the possibility of federal prisoners getting furloughs.
Combined with Reagan's demonization of drugs, certainly the
chances of me getting a quick peek at the outside before I was to be
released seemed nonexistent. But because the U.S. Bureau of Prisons
had violated its own rules and guidelines in transferring level 1 (the
lowest security designation) prisoners from Lompoc Prison Camp to
the medium to high security level prison at Terminal Island Federal
Penitentiary, the warden unexpectedly granted me a five-day
furlough within six months of my release date.

A friend bought me round-trip tickets from Long Beach to San
Francisco and my only concern was getting back to the Bay Area
without incident. But, as with many of my concerns in life, it was not
to be. I told the ticket agent at the airport that a ticket was there
under my name. "No problem," she replied, "I'll just need some
identification."

Under normal circumstances, one would merely produce a driver's
license but I had none. In fact, all I had was a carbon copy of my
prison release papers issued for my furlough. Already things were
going awry and only because I had no alternative did I show her the
papers. Nervously I watched her reaction as she read them. She then
looked up at me and smiled. "Family ties, huh?" Family ties was the
excuse given on my release papers in order to justify a furlough. The
real reason, of course, was to end years of celibacy.

"Let's see if we can get you a seat next to a woman." Her
unexpected support seemed to be a hopeful portent of what was to

come. But after checking seat availability, she continued, "I'm sorry, no such luck. I'll have to seat you between two men."

I thanked her for her concern, telling her everything was all right, that the last time I had to take an assigned seat I was put next to a great looking hooker. She laughed, wished me luck in strengthening family ties, and handed me my ticket.

Many things had changed in the five years I had been in prison. For one thing, the seats on airplanes had become noticeably smaller and cramped. I took my seat, buckled my seat belt, and closed my eyes in order to meditate and lessen the chances of any contact with those on either side of me.

As the plane took off, I could feel the familiar sense of relaxation and peace that meditation brings. I knew I would need it as the readjustment to the outside world was not going to be easy. Then I heard the voice, not God's, but a human one, coming from the person seated on my left.

"Do you live in San Francisco?"

I couldn't believe the temerity of the person. It was obvious my eyes were closed. How could he be so thoughtless? I ignored him, believing he would get the hint, but it didn't work.

"Hello." This time the voice was louder, more insistent, "Do you live in San Francisco?"

That did it. I decided to end his one sided conversation once and for all. I opened my eyes to see who it was. He was skinny, with glasses, in his mid-twenties.

"No, I don't live in San Francisco," I hissed dangerously, "I live in prison and I'm on my way to San Francisco on a furlough."

The barely-contained rage in my voice could not be mistaken. I glared at him and once again closed my eyes, convinced the dialogue was over. I was wrong. The voice intruded again.

"I have a book about that."

This was too much. I opened my eyes and saw the reason for his thoughtlessness. On his lap was a now-opened Bible. He looked at me expectantly, ready to share the good news of Christ's arrival with a stranger.

"I think prison sentences should be longer," he continued. "I'm a Christian. This book explains many things."

I don't know who else heard what I said but at that point I didn't care. I was enraged at his statement about longer prison sentences. Some of my friends were doing twenty and forty years and even life.

"Just because you call yourself a Christian doesn't mean you are one," I retorted, livid with anger. "You have no right to call yourself a Christian. You know nothing of Christ or His love. All you know is judgment. If you had met the woman at the well, you would've called the cops on her. You aren't worthy of His name."

Again, I closed my eyes, signaling the end of the conversation. I couldn't believe it. This unexpected intrusion from a self-anointed and so-called born again Christian had turned my furlough into the furlough from hell. Shaking with rage, I tried to regain my center, needing to reconnect with something other than the self-righteous opinions and judgments of my self-anointed born-again seatmate.

After a while, I sank again into a meditative state and I became calmer. But, then, in the midst of my newly-regained peace, I heard his voice, again.

"You're right. I don't know anything about love. I just prayed to God thanking him for sending you to me."

I opened my eyes, amazed at what he had just said.

"If you mean that," I eventually replied, "then you have a chance to find out who Christ is. He's about love, and judgment has nothing to do with love. I hope you find out the difference."

And then I closed my eyes, hoping the rest of the trip to San Francisco would be uneventful.

My friend Thomas picked me up at the airport, and I told him to head for Chinatown before dropping me off at a girlfriend's apartment. I wanted a roast duck rice plate, something else I hadn't had in five years. I told him about my encounter on the airplane and I could see his rage as I told him what had happened.

"That little punk gave it up that easy?" he retorted angrily. "You should've asked him for his car keys and his wallet and told him to send you $50 a month until you got out."

I smiled. I was home again. The roast duck was good and the family ties would be even better.

Most of those who say they are reborn are not.
They are only hoping. Yearning, however, is a
place to start.

Until seen for the self-embraced shadow it is,
Guilt, at best, is only in remission

Just as ontogeny recapitulates phylogeny
So too does experience recapitulate guilt
Fear is the cotter pin of guilt's judgment
Experience this fear of guilt and experience the truth of fear
Experience the truth of fear and experience the existence of truth
Life recapitulates love

THE JOURNEY AND THE GYPSY GIRL
OR
HOW MONKEY DISCOVERED THE TRUE TREASURE OF
THE GOLD MOUNTAIN

PART I

I went to see a Gypsy girl
When I was seventeen
I heard she had a crystal ball
In which tomorrow could be seen

I lived in California then
In a suburb way too small
For what was about to happen
The sixties if you recall

She had a scarf wrapped 'round her head
Her fingers were covered with rings
A golden circle pierced her nose
And her trailer was filled with things

That a boy such as I would never see
In a nice suburban house
Crosses, incense, and pentagrams
Were next to chairs and couch

Well, the Gypsy girl, she looked at me
With eyes that seemed to know
That my thoughts were on her blouse so full
That hung so very low

And with a smile she sat me down
In front of her crystal ball
She said she was born in Romania
With a gift that could tell me all

Her price she said was twenty-five bucks
Which was more than I possessed
But she took the fifteen that was in my hand
And said I could owe the rest

Now, dear sir, do you really want
Me, your fortune to tell?
For oftentimes, it's best left alone
For you never know how well

You can handle a future that will surely be
At odds with what you believe
So, please be certain, before we proceed
The truth you're willing to receive

Well, all I wanted to know back then
If a dentist I would be
Orthodontia seemed a perfect choice
For a person such as me

She closed her eyes and I wondered what
Was passing through her mind
Next, she stared right through my head
Seeing what she could find

She said I know you're young and filled with hopes
That I know will never be
But you've paid my price, and come to me
With a request for you to see

For unknown reasons I can only see
Your life till forty-four
But for fifteen down and ten bucks owed
You could hardly hope for more

At forty-four, you'll be folding clothes
Inside a prison laundry
For a man you'll know as Big Bird
And there's something else I see

Before that job, in prison too,
You'll work as a garbage man
Taking care of people's trash
And dumping out their cans

But you'll have traveled much of the world by then
Seeing Paris, Rome, Beijing
You'll have slept in places such as Marrakech
And stayed in Medellin

But your greatest journey will be an inward one
To the center of your very soul
You'll discover the truths you've always sought
And you'll learn to rock 'n roll

She smiled at me, took my hands in hers,
And her hands were oh so hot
She said Let tomorrow come when'er it will
And accept what can't be bought

She laughed when she saw me hesitate
And said that she already knew
I wasn't yet ready for a Gypsy girl's love
And the freedom I wanted then too

It's been awhile since I've thought of her
That day and what she said
Cause it's all come true, every word of it,
And it seems that I've been led

On a journey far greater than a dentist's chair
And a home and a condo or two
And I wait for the rest to unfold when it will
And for that freedom the Gypsy girl knew

———————————

On the leeward side of Kuaui is a resort hotel that faces a perfect crescent shaped beach. That beach, composed of fine white sand, is bordered by rows of tall graceful palms. When I first discovered the beach and the resort built around it, I knew I had discovered something special. Its beauty rivaled the aquamarine pools and waterfalls on the Havasupai Indian reservation in Arizona, and that of a particular sunset I had seen from a suite at the Hassler Hotel overlooking the Spanish Steps in Rome, while on LSD.

I was fortunate to have stayed at that resort, the Waiohai on Poipu Beach, a number of times before it was torn down and rebuilt in order to meet the expanding needs of a changing world. The venerable Waiohai was not the first nor will it be the last resort to fall victim to the inexorable sword of change, and I was fortunate enough, I believe, to have missed its transition in 1977.

Here, however, in June of 1990 I am eyewitness to the passing of another era as another destination resort—albeit a resort of a different type—passes from the scene. Known as Club Fed in acknowledgment of its media concocted reputation for prison-ease, Lompoc Federal Prison Camp has now become a Federal Correctional Institution. Its once open borders are now surrounded by rows of high fencing topped by rolls upon rolls of knife sharp razor wire, and its golf course built for Republican Watergate politico H.R. Haldeman is a relic of the past—if indeed it had ever truly existed. I, myself, never saw the golf course and it is entirely possible that its existence, at best, was only a rumor.

This week, the last in June, signals my having completed forty-five months of my sentence here at Lompoc. Because of my propensities toward the written word, numerous fellow inmates have suggested that I write of the unique experience encountered here at the Camp. In the past, I chose not to do so because I felt I had nothing significant to say; but now, however, after forty-five months I do have some thoughts.

Today is the Fourth of July 1990. This day in America is celebrated as a holiday just as during the horror years of the Spanish inquisition the Roman Catholic Church continued to celebrate

Christmas in honor of the birth of Christ. Such holidays keep people and leaders in touch with dates and events that once had actual significance. I myself believe that once upon the Earth there walked the true son of GOD. I believe too that once upon a time the leaders of the United States of America actually believed in the principles upon which this nation was founded.

Twenty-one years ago, on another Fourth of July, I was released from the county jail facility in San Francisco, California. The year was 1969. The end of the 60s—an era that was to have a formative and lasting effect on my life. My sentence at that time was for the illegal (what a concept) sales of lysergic acid di-ethyl amide-25, or LSD. What a drug. What an era. What a life.

In the fall of 1966, I had entered Hastings College of the Law in San Francisco. One year later, I had taken LSD, was living in the Haight-Ashbury, and was running a food concession at the Family Dog's Avalon Ballroom on Sutter Street. There, from Thursday through Sunday nights, bands such as Big Brother and the Holding Company, the Quicksilver Messenger Service, and the Grateful Dead would play. In those days the hippies in San Francisco would often hang out on a hill in Golden Gate Park known as Hippie Hill.

When I first arrived here at Lompoc Federal Prison Camp, a hill covered with tall eucalyptus trees was known by the very same name, a metal-sculpted psychedelic amanita muscaria mushroom adding another connection between those two hills and those two eras. Now that hill is outside the newly erected fence that surrounds this prison. Hippie Hill, like the freedoms upon which this country was founded, has become but a memory—a memory we now see through prison fencing and razor wire.

My thoughts regarding this transition are reflected in a letter I wrote to my son this last January. He had asked for my thoughts regarding the American flag for a speech he was preparing for a high school oratory contest. My letter to him is as follows:

January 18, 1990

Dear Benjamin:

As I look back, I've come to the conclusion that the American flag meant the same to my generation as it did to others— freedom, love of GOD, country, etc. That it no longer does so is a result of generational experiences that our generation alone has gone through.

That those of your grandfather's generation hold the flag in high regard is to be expected. To them, the flag represents a country, though perhaps not perfect, that embodies the highest and noblest aspirations of mankind. Heir to the doctrine of individual rights embodied in the Magna Carta and stated so simply in the Declaration of Independence and Bill of Rights, the United States of America was born of an age-old dream of a life free from the meddling of capricious tyrannies in the form of landed gentry, royalty, and others who would believe that their birthright, wealth, and power made them somehow better than their fellow man.

The United States' form of government, a democracy, was not a new concept in the history of humanity. The Greek city-states, pre-dating the Roman Empire, engaged in such exercises and more recently, the cantons (city-states) of Switzerland since the 13th century have used democratic methods of voting to determine their political choices.

What was however unique to the American experiment was its explicit circumscription of governmental powers vis-a-vis those whom it purported to serve. The founding fathers created a government to serve the people and most importantly and uniquely in the Bill of Rights gave the individual INALIENABLE rights and powers regarding the government that was created to serve him or her.

Now, two hundred years later the Bill of Rights is in shambles and the right to bail and laws prohibiting illegal searches,

91

seizures, and detainers are so compromised as to exist only as words on paper, not as the tangible rights of a citizenry. Ironically, in this day and age governmental intrusion is not the result of the economic power of a landed gentry or the created birthright of royalty; it exists as an extension of the whims of a democratically-elected majority.

Democracy is a method of choosing destinies where groups of people are concerned. It alone is no guarantee of the rights of mankind as stated in the Declaration of Independence and Bill of Rights. Indeed, the eradication of Jews, Gypsies, and Homosexuals in pre-war Germany was supported by a democratically-elected government just as the making and breaking of treaties with the pre-existing Native American Indian populations was done with the tacit consent of the democratically-elected governments of the United States.

Now, under the symbol of the American flag, my generation has witnessed the rape of the Bill of Rights by a democratically-elected majority. Today, the people and the United States government view the Bill of Rights as an impediment to the governmental exercise of power. Indeed, that is so. Indeed, that is why it was created.

Those who hold the flag dear understand little of what this means. For them, the flag represents a country that gave them a chance to make a living in a world capricious and ungiving. My generation acknowledges that. We see why and how those who purport to love the U.S. and its flag do so. We also see that the American experiment is over, finished, a failure; that words on paper are no safeguards; that tyrants can be composed of taxpayers, good citizens, and those that call themselves Christians as well as thugs and bullies, rich and wealthy landowners, and those born of royal blood.

The desire to force others to act and behave as one wishes is no longer the unique domain of kings. Two hundred years after the issuance of the Bill of Rights and the Declaration of Independence, it is all too clear that the desire to dictate by governmental fiat is alive and well in the souls of the average United States citizen.

Ironically, I, one generation before, had entered that very same competition in which my son was now competing. In 1960, I had reached the Western Region Finals of the Lion's Club Oratory Contest. There, I echoed the words of Franklin Roosevelt stating that our generation, too, had a rendezvous with destiny.

Little did I know in 1960 what was destined. For our generation had not yet embarked on the journey that was to make Mr. Toad's Wild Ride seem like a valium induced stupor. Indeed, it was not the drug valium that we took on that wild wild ride. It was instead a drug called LSD. A drug that unbuckled our seat belts instead of securing them. A drug that gave our generation a glimpse of eternal truths instead of the suburban trophies that lay in front of us. A drug that the CIA had inadvertently introduced to America's youth. For that introduction, on behalf of all those who have benefited by its gifts, I would now like to say thank you to the CIA.

I want to say thank you to the CIA
Those covert boys of the American way
'Cause without their help to keep America strong
I never would've learned what's right from wrong

The story begins after World War II
When the Nazis were down but the red, white, and blue
Had a war to fight with a new enemy
Commies they were who wanted to free
The whole wide world from the capitalists' grip
They blamed the bankers for the world's bad trip

Well, the USA decided to fight
This Communist threat with all its might
So the CIA, who we know to be
The so-called friend of liberty

Had this bright idea of how to chill
The Communist threat with a brand new pill

Inside the pill was LSD
A brand new drug they thought could be
A secret weapon for Commie spies
An antidote for their Bolshevik lies

Well to find out what this drug could do
They needed someone to give it to
So they got some prisoners in Lexington
Doing time for heroin

For seventy straight days they blew their minds
With LSD to find the line
That would drive them over to insanity
To freak them out to keep America free

Well it now appeared the U.S. had
A drug that was truly truly bad
So next they gave it to the mentally ill
Just to see just how well

The ill could cope when blown away
The doctors had a field day
Colleges next gave LSD
To students so professors could see

How LSD could truly be used
In the cold cold war and not abused
But as the students took it one by one
To their shock they found it was fun

Their minds were open, suddenly clear
Of personal, social, and cultural fear
They started to smile, their hair grew long
They gave up shoes for beads and thongs

They took off their clothes, danced in the sun
Put down their books and had some fun
Make love not war was what they said
As they rocked out to the Grateful Dead

The acid was coming in many forms
Flooding all those college dorms
Cubes, white flats, and colored tabs
And anything else Stanley Owsley had

Owsley had learned to make LSD
So we could try it, Americans like me
At that time I was going to school
To be a lawyer to learn the rules

That made this country great and free
Giving freedom to you and me
But the country freaked when the hippies came
'Cause they thought we'd gone insane

They didn't know the CIA
Was making it safe for the American way
So they sent the cops to stop the fun
With handcuffs, warrants, jails, and guns

It's been some time, those days have gone
The '60s they're called, off and on
By those who remember a time long past
When a dream appeared that wouldn't last

Of a world new and so far out
A world free of fear and doubt
Where brothers and sisters could sing and dance
Where love was given another chance

And although I'm now in prison here
My inner self can still yet hear
That eternal dream so far away
That was brought to me by the CIA

It is not possible to truly understand what exactly happened during the 1960s. There was so much LSD there is a saying, if you remember the '60s, you weren't there. Yet, the questions remain. Why did a generation decide to act out a live psychedelic version of "The Body Snatchers" right in front of their parents? What caused this specific generation to become so estranged that the parent culture has now reacted so violently as to erect a police state complete with paid informants and coercive judicial proceedings to regain its sense of control and order? Maybe it was Mad Magazine. Maybe it was the fluoridated water supply. Maybe it was humankind struggling to free itself from age-old guilts and constrictions...maybe.

The Grateful Dead once sang the words "What a long strange trip it's been." I've had time here at Lompoc Federal Prison Camp to think about those events between then and now, between the 1960s and the 1990s, between law school and this ten-year prison sentence. Last year I reflected on this long strange journey and although life has not been what I expected, it has been far far greater than anything I would have chosen on my own. At the time, I wrote the following essay describing some of those thoughts.

JOURNEYS

Life itself can be described as a
journey and although it is not always a
vacation, it is certainly always a trip.

This morning, munching on some trail mix, I came at last to the travel section of the Sunday newspaper. Always my favorite section, it was reserved for last—a welcome respite from the news that usually preceded it. This Sunday's edition was to be no exception. There, descriptions of exotic destinations filled its pages. Reading the articles rekindled memories of places I had been and thoughts of those I had still to visit.

My own journey had taken me far from the scenes of my childhood. In the 1950s and amongst the flat and endless stretches of tract and custom homes, Tower Records and Shakey's Pizza Parlor, I and many others gestated in prototypical suburban petri dishes throughout the United States. There, little league, piano lessons, two-car garages, and yearly subscriptions to National Geographic and Sunset magazines were to be however inadequate portents or preparation for what was about to be. The 1960s, an era that caught everyone unawares, would erupt from a somnambulism that would give no warning. To journey, however, one need not be forewarned. One need only to go.

Go, I did. At the time, the going seemed less by choice than by circumstance. Now I know time and circumstance are predetermined by fate; then, I did not. The journey, beginning in the raw ignorance of American suburbia, was to take me through the self-righteous anger and bitterness of the anti-war era, and through much of the phenomena that were to affect or afflict this nation's then youth. Had I known then the journey's itinerary, I would not have started. However, I did not, so I did go and now, having gone, regret nothing of what the journey has had to teach.

Travel to faraway places was not high on the agenda of my youth. But, then again, the agenda of my generation was a hidden one and irrespective of what we perhaps hoped it to be— certainly it was to turn out differently. Shattered marriages, drugs that opened, drugs that closed, and hopes rising only to fall, leaving behind a darkness intensified by the light which had preceded it was nothing we had expected or wanted.

Then, how would I have known or even imagined that someday I would mount a camel on the Great Wall of China, or watch in horror as the San Francisco Tactical Squad chased and brutally beat defenseless hippies, and then walk past that same squad fifteen years later when invited to the Mayor's reception for the President of France and remember that scene of rage and fear from years before. Inner Mongolia, Marrakech, Morocco, Presidential invitations and waist chains and leg irons on the way to federal prison were all to be a part of what lay ahead, at least for me.

These were events and places unimaginable to a teenage boy growing up in the suburbs of the 1950s—a world as buttressed against chaos as was the palace of the Buddha's boyhood. But like his world, that world too was to disintegrate in the face of forces our parents strove with all their might and power to keep out.

But what else could not be imagined was that out of that chaos, out of that disintegration, would evolve a peace and power as unexpected as it was initially unsought. It is only lately I have realized that the journey of our generation is not yet over; in truth, it has only just begun.

THE SUN AND THE MOON ARE ONE AND HOW HE GOT HIS NAME is a story I wrote while here at Lompoc Federal Prison Camp. I often reread it as "I wait for the rest to unfold when it will and for that freedom the Gypsy girl knew."

THE SUN AND THE MOON ARE ONE
AND HOW HE GOT HIS NAME

I was very young when I heard THE SUN AND THE MOON ARE ONE tell the story of how he got his name. He was old, much older than we were but we all understood what he said. Often, elders speak in ways the young do not understand; not so with THE SUN AND THE MOON ARE ONE. All of us who listened that day understood perfectly.

Why he spoke to us was something we did not understand. He said that he wished to speak to us before our skies clouded over. He said that this would happen to us when we were older; but now, as children, with our skies still clear, we would understand the words he would say. And later, just as he said, our skies did cloud over. But that day, we understood and this, to the best of my recollection, is what he said:

When I was, like you are now, a child, my name was Strong Mind. And, like you, I did not know how I got my name. The name, Strong Mind, had been given to me like yours have been given to you. When my name was called, I answered. When it was used, I knew they were speaking of me.

My childhood, like that of all children, was filled with the river of growing up. And as my river flowed, I learned. For that is what the river of growing up does for all of us. It flows, it teaches; and, as it teaches, we learn.

As children, our worlds were new and our skies were clear. But as the river of growing up filled us, our worlds began to change. We learned that all things, like us, had names and that all names were separate and apart. That the tree and the earth that grew it were not the same nor were the sky or the clouds or the sun or the moon.

As we were filled, we never questioned what we were learning. We never asked whether the lessons of the river of growing up were, in fact, true. We were only children then, as you are children now.

Soon, we found that our worlds had changed. Our lives were no longer fun and joyful adventures. We had become burdened with problems and struggles. So this is the final lesson of the river of growing up, we thought. So this is truly how life is.

We were wrong, however. There was yet another lesson the river had to teach, and that is why I am here today. Perhaps by telling you now, while your skies are still clear, you will remember my words and you will continue to learn and continue to move even when your skies cloud over and your world seems to have forever changed.

THE SUN AND THE MOON ARE ONE is not a name. It is a truth. Names are not truths, they are only names and names are only labels. Someday, you will discover you are the TRUTH. And, on that day, you will notice that your sky is clear once again.

THE JOURNEY & THE GYPSY GIRL
OR
HOW MONKEY DISCOVERED THE TRUE TREASURE OF
THE GOLD MOUNTAIN
PART II

In August of 1990, I was transferred from Lompoc Federal Correctional Institution to a federal prison in San Pedro, California. Located on an island in the middle of a harbor, Terminal Island Federal Correctional Institution truly belongs in Southern California. T.I., as it is known, resembles an old style prison with its gun towers and its north and south prison yards.

Still, T.I. possesses an air that is pure Southern California. Because Terminal Island's south yard opens directly onto the water, we convicts could watch through double rows of barbed razor wire as pleasure craft and tour boats circled the harbor. And as they went by, we could hear the tour boats interminably repeat the history of Terminal Island. And as we and the tourists listened, we would observe each other with a similar curiosity; for to us, a world of afternoon pleasure boating was as unreal as a world of isolated incarceration was to them.

Fronting the Pacific Ocean were the stately homes of the warden and assistant wardens, the grounds of which I and other inmates were assigned to maintain. And one day, as I and two other convicts watched, a tour boat came into view. On its rear deck stood a solitary black man. As the boat passed, the man, upon seeing us, raised his arm and clenched his fist in a spontaneous salute of solidarity and understanding. And the three of us, as one, returned the gesture. I will never forget that day and what that man's salute meant. I will also never forget those I met in prison and the nature of the time I passed there with them. After one month at Terminal Island, I wrote the following verses:

Can you do time?
Can you live a life?
Can you do it on your own?
Alone just like a knife

That cuts through the darkness
Of the hell of being alone
Can you do it straight boy?
Without being stoned?

Can you do it boy?
Can you do it boy?
Oh yeah oh yeah
Can you do it boy?

Do you need another
To make it through the night?
To hold you close to tell you
That everything's all right

When you know inside you
Deep inside your soul
That the words ain't true
That it really ain't so

Too afraid to let go
Of what can never be
Too afraid to look around
Afraid what you might see

But the fear ain't real
But you'll never know that's true
Until you quit your runnin' boy
From the fear inside of you

Can you do it boy?
Can you do it boy?
Oh yeah oh yeah
Can you do it boy?

When one is in prison, the question of being able to do the time is rhetorical for one must do what one must do. Doing time is not easy but somehow, day by day, it still gets done. There was a joke making the rounds when I first got to T.I. and it went something like this:

A judge has just sentenced a twenty-year-old kid to forty years and the kid protests,

"Your honor, I can't do forty years."

The judge looks down at the young boy and says,

"Well, you just do what you can and we'll help you with the rest."

Since Terminal Island was a medium security to high security prison, the sentences being served there were much longer than those at Lompoc camp. Instead of six months or four to five years, sentences of twenty to forty years were not uncommon and I knew more than one person doing life. The racial make-up at Terminal Island also was different. There were far more Blacks and Hispanics than at Lompoc, and it was clear that the lower one's racial group was on the economic food chain, the more at risk were its members.

Downside economics, however, played only a minor role in my becoming involved in what society calls "criminal behavior". My coming of age in America had been criminalized from the very beginning. The 1960s were a tumultuous period of social conflict and consequent disorder. And the laws and the order that society then attempted to impose were clearly on the side of others than myself.

We already knew that to protest racism and the war in Vietnam would result in being branded un-American and being investigated by the FBI. Consequently, the fact that the government also subsequently criminalized our lifestyle in addition to our political beliefs didn't surprise us at all. Our politics and lifestyles were already outside the mainstream of American society; and by the end of the 1960s, we didn't need a civics class to know we too were outlaws.

It was clear to us that the criminalization of our drugs was a result of a society which had already criminalized our behavior and our beliefs. Our drugs, deemed illegal, were certainly no more socially catastrophic than their drugs, alcohol and tobacco, deemed legal.

> They drink their Johnny Walker
> And smoke cigars by the fire
> While cancer and cirrhosis
> Help most of them retire

Tobacco and alcohol are directly responsible for the deaths of 500,000 Americans a year while deaths from all illegal drugs combined amount to less then 5,000 annually. Nonetheless, while we are imprisoned and our assets seized, the American tobacco industry enjoys strong political support and hypocriti-cally remains one of the primary contributors to the Partnership for a Drug-Free America. Justice in America, at least for those in mainstream America, means exactly what it says—just us.

> Marijuana cocaine
> Nicotine and booze
> No one said they're good for you
> But it's we who cannot choose

When I was younger, I believed that the role of government was to protect the economic and civil liberties of its citizens and their right to choose. It is now obvious that I was mistaken. Government instead functions according to the golden rule; to wit, those who have the gold rule. And we, young and having no gold at all, were completely powerless before those who did.

We are Americans
And Americans are free
Free to pursue happiness
Justice and liberty

The American way gives all the right
To do as they may choose
The American way don't discriminate
Between pot cocaine and booze

And just 'cause uptight citizens
With prune lips for a face
Don't like the things we like to do
Don't make us no disgrace

Von Mises said before he died
That freedom was the key
That freedom would allow us
To unlock our destiny

Now I was born in America
In Washington DC
The capitol of a land
That's never been quite free

And until we let each other
Live as they would be
Freedom's just another word
For what is tyranny

For when the law is used to force
Others into line
It's one against another
For justice is not blind

We are Americans
Americans are free
Free to pursue happiness
Justice and liberty

Americans are free. Free to pursue happiness, justice, and liberty. Sure. Just try it and see what happens.

Those who do have the power in America certainly did not like us. They mistook our opposition to the Vietnam War for an attack on America's values. But they were wrong. Our opposition to the Vietnam War was based on the belief that America stood for freedom and democracy and South Vietnam was anything but that. South Vietnam was a French colonial remnant ruled by a corrupt military dictatorship backed by the CIA. To those of us who opposed the war, the idea of American blood being shed in support of a corrupt totalitarian regime was an affront to everything this country stood for. To us, now and then, it is not we, but those who supported the war, who did the real disservice to America.

This country never forgave us for our opposition to that war. They blamed America's defeat on us then as they were to blame America's social ills on us later. The Republicans especially never forgave us. But that is to be expected, for the Republicans represent the rich and powerful in America and in America it is the rich and powerful who rule. They who have the gold rule and, in the 1980s, they certainly ruled.

In the spring of 1990, after having observed an unbroken decade under Republican leadership, I was moved to make the following observations.

Republicans are caring
They are people too
They care about so many things
They don't know what to do

They care about poverty
The destitute and poor
They care about minorities
And wonder how much more

Tax dollars it may cost
Helping those in dire need
They care about their money
They care about their greed

They care about the homeless
The need that they are in
So millions of tax dollars
They proceeded then to skim

With kickbacks and consulting fees
They stole from those in need
HUD just gave Republicans
A trough in which to feed

They care about democracy
They care for freedom's fight
They care about humanity
They care about human rights

But when there is a conflict
Over power and what's right
The Republicans choose power
And quickly leave the fight

For remember in El Salvador
The murder of the priests
Our Republicans then in power
Provided no relief

And they did the same with China
With their stand on human rights
Where poets are imprisoned
For cryin' in the night

Where innocents are slaughtered
For the right to speak their mind
Where people are coerced
To toe a party line

But America's Republicans
Care for many things
And power is first among them
Not the rights of human beings

But Republicans are caring
They are people too
They care about so many things
They don't know what to do

Of course, Republicans do not see themselves this way. Self-esteem is not a problem for those who mistakenly believe their wealth and power is testimony to their worth as human beings. Nonetheless, twelve years of Republican rule from 1980-1992 did fundamental damage to America's freedoms.

The Republican demand for law and order was but a smokescreen for the dismantling of individual rights on an unprecedented scale. Using the war against drugs as an excuse to strengthen the police powers of the state, the Republicans proceeded to strip away all constitutional safeguards for individual rights during the 1980s. Watching this process, I used to joke that someday the Constitutional prohibition against cruel and unusual punishment would be tossed out on the grounds that cruelty in our system no longer is unusual.

This attempt at humor unfortunately turned out to be true. In 1991, Antonin Scalia, a right-wing Republican appointee to the Supreme Court, denied a new trial for a young black man sentenced to over twenty years for possessing a small amount of rock cocaine. Scalia wrote that although the twenty-year sentence may indeed be cruel, such sentences in America are not unusual.

Scalia, you are heartless
In your black Supreme Court robes
For you serve the darker forces
That persecuted Job

But with your Latin learning
And your law books at your side
You will someday face your judgments
From GOD you cannot hide

For Christ Himself said those words
That you will someday know
That as you do to the least of men
You do to Him also

The law today is neither just nor merciful. It reflects not the lofty
ideals of the Constitution and the Bill of Rights. It reflects instead
the meanness and prejudices of those charged with interpreting it.
What is cruel is no longer unusual, and the courts today are less a
forum for redress than they are instruments of coercion. These are
dark days in America. So, too, were those of its beginning. Whether
this is its end remains to be seen, for the war against crime and drugs
is not yet over.

Lying on my prison bunk
The Band's on the radio
Memories of times long past
Come with the rock 'n roll

And I wonder what has happened
To the dreams of yesterday
When everything seemed so far out
That we only lived to play

Now my heart is full and heavy
As the hopes of yesteryear
Have turned to fear and worry
'bout what is happenin' here

We thought perhaps things had changed
A world free at last
From the guilt fear and oppression
That had ruled us in the past

But they hadn't really gone away
They were still there deep inside
Where we wouldn't let them reach us
And now we cannot hide

The prison guards listen to rock 'n roll
And I wonder what they hear
It cannot be the beat I know
It's something else I fear

The winds are ill they bode no good
Evil's on the rise
But the way this world's always been
It comes as no surprise

My heart's now full and heavy
As the hopes of yesteryear
Have turned to fear and worry
'bout what is happenin' here

What is happening today in America was predicted over a hundred and fifty years ago by Alexis De Tocqueville. In his landmark book, **Democracy In America**, De Tocqueville in 1835 predicted that American democracy could someday turn to tyranny. Indeed, that is exactly what has happened. And since it is a tyranny imposed by the majority over a minority, its existence will be denied by the majority that imposes it. Denied or not, it is tyranny nonetheless.

Police state
1984
Police state
1984

1984 it came
It never went away
1984's still here
It's called the USA

The Constitution and Bill of Rights
No longer are in force
For history in the USA
Has gone another course

With snitches warrants lies 'n guns
They've filled the prisons full
They call it law and order
But that's a crock of bull

Its real name is tyranny
Disguised by laws and books
Its purpose is oppression folks
So take another look

They speak of God and justice and
Their churches they are filled
With symbols of Christ Jesus
Whose spirit they have killed

The scales of blind justice
Are weighted down with gold
And the votes of politicians
Are freely bought and sold

They said it would not happen
It could not happen here
A police state where the people
Are ruled by guns and fear

But while you watched the sitcoms
And football on TV
They killed the Constitution and
No longer are you free

Police state
1984
Police state
1984

Americans, at least those at the top of the economic food chain, have little understanding how their actions affect those beneath them. America is an economic hierarchy where those on the bottom have been dispossessed of everything except handguns, despair, and ammunition. To wonder why America is experiencing such widespread violence is akin to an alcoholic wondering why his liver is failing. Crime today has America tightly in its grip. And like the creditor whose largest debtor is more his master than servant, until America comes to grips with the actuality of what ails it, it will continue to be torn by a conflict it can neither understand nor solve.

Anger seeps throughout this land
Hate, frustration, rage, the man
Compassion belongs to yesterday
Republicans rule the selfish way

Pick on someone not your size
Granada, Panama, more white lies
The nation's mood cries for blood
Who's to blame? S & L's and HUD

The media fans the nation's rage
Blacks still victims of this age
Another enemy has been found
The Japanese are still around

For years the U.S. owned it all
Other countries at our beck and call
Someone else now has the dollars
Now it's us who scream and holler

B-2 bombers, billions for war
The enemy's gone but Republicans want more
The poor and homeless have no voice
The rich are saying that it's by choice

Safe behind double locked doors
Minorities hired to do their chores
The rich get richer and the poor stay broke
Life is fair the Republicans joke

The prison experience is a harsh, psychologically brutal, separating experience. Cut off from the world at large, from loved ones, from family and friends, the prison world becomes the only world that exists. I was fortunate, however, that this forced isolation gave me a needed opportunity—the opportunity to be with myself.

I was fortunate in other respects as well. In prison I watched as kids entered Terminal Island Penitentiary with more time to do than the years they had lived. They were but youths whose entire adult lives were now taken away. Most of them had only known poverty, the streets, and the dangerous games they had played to escape them. Myself, by the time I received my ten-year sentence, I had already seen much of what the world had to offer. The Gypsy girl had been right. At forty years of age I had already

Traveled much of the world by then
Seeing Paris, Rome, Beijing
I'd already slept in places such as Marrakech
And stayed in Medellin

In many ways, I was ready for prison and what it could offer the few such as me. Prison for me was the monastery I would never have entered on my own. As it was, it took the U.S. government to force me to leave what was familiar in order to find what had been lost.

I know what the prophets were saying
I know the meaning of runes
I know the mystery of ages
Learned in the sands of the dunes

I've stayed in the hotels of Paris
I've slept in cold prison cells
I know what mankind calls heaven
I know what mankind calls hell

And I care not what others might think
Of my actions my life and my loves
For what I do on the planes of the earth
Is between me and YOU up above

YOU brought me back to your table
YOU gave me a house of my own
YOU gave me permission to live and to learn
YOU gave me the freedom to roam

Your children know not the love of your heart
Your children know not your face
They search in memories far from your light
They pray to images they've put in your place

But me YOU guided in darkness
Out of the wilderness of my own thoughts
YOU showed me the truth in the thickets
Thickets in which I'd been caught

And now I'm as free as the eagle
That flies in the skies overhead
I'm free which is what YOU intended
Why else would I YOU have led

We shall see what the future will bring me
What for me YOU now have in store
I'm willing to do what needs to be done
Whether in peace or whether in war

Your hand I can see is now moving
Your words have reached my ears
Your cautions now I am heeding
I am learning to love even fear

113

I treasure what once was buried
By I who knew it not
The secret of all the ages
The secret which I YOU have taught

YOU brought me back to your table
YOU gave me a house of my own
YOU gave me permission to live and to learn
YOU gave me the freedom to roam

Thankfulness is a state that is truly blessed. I consider myself blessed in that I can say I am thankful for my journey which included a significant stretch in prison. Few can say that and few should. I am thankful that I can.

I am thankful that for the most part I have worked through the rage, anger, and fear that resulted from my experiences. I believe that had I not taken LSD in the 1960s, my rage could very well have destroyed me. LSD radically refocused and rechanneled my energies at that critical juncture in my life.

It left my feelings untouched, however, and it took my prison experience to bring them back so they could be accepted, experienced, and understood. Feelings suppressed and avoided are nonetheless still there and they will find a way to manifest themselves. In the 1980s, the Republicans came back to finish what they had begun twenty years before. To my surprise, this time I grew from the encounter.

Life hurts deep inside us
Closed off and far away
It seems there's nothing we can do
It seems there's nothing we can say

Questions are unanswered
Doubts and fears abound
Everyone is paralyzed
No one makes a sound

People acting normal
Hoping fear will leave
People dying everywhere
Life is like a sieve

Couples holding on
To each other for dear life
Holding on so tightly
They drain each other's life

Afraid of letting go
Afraid of being alone
Trying different churches
Trying being stoned

The pain is growing larger
Asking to be felt
So check the cards you're holding
And watch what's being dealt

For we can't avoid forever
Our feelings deep inside
There's nowhere we can go
There's nowhere we can hide

Life hurts deep inside us
Closed off and far away
It seems there's nothing we can do
It seems there's nothing we can say

The winds will soon be blowing
Through everybody's life
Changes and upheaval
Cutting like a knife

Through the walls that we've erected
Around the pain that's deep inside
Releasing now forever
The hurts we've tried to hide

But after we have felt
The hurts that are so deep
At long long last we'll heal
And no longer will we weep

For underneath the pain
That's been frozen for so long
GOD's hand is reaching towards us
For to GOD we do belong

I am thankful too for my family and friends that were there during this separation. It was difficult for them and I know it was for me. Only those imprisoned and those who care for them can truly know how difficult it is. But as difficult as this journey was for us, this journey was perhaps hardest on our parents.

It was just the other morning
I heard a song being sung
The words were full of bitterness
And spoke of hopes undone

It could have been your parents
Or maybe it was mine
But beneath their words of anger
I thought I heard them crying

These are the words I heard that night
I hear them still today
You've heard them too I think my friend
For they will not go away

They said you should've done the things
Exactly as you were told
But no you didn't listen then
Instead you rock 'n rolled

Now look at what has happened
Because you had some fun
Your life it is in shambles
Because of what you've done

Well I listened to their words that night
To all they had to say
And I can't say that I blame them much
For why they feel that way

But I do not think they understand
The need to feel free
To act in spite of guilt and fear
The need to finally be

Just what you are, the simple truth
So you can go from there
And find the other truths that are
That lead to places where

You know at last you are the child
Of a GOD who holds you dear
For it's a truth you'll never know
When you're trapped in guilt and fear

I was fortunate that I had the opportunity to reunite with my mother and father after my time in prison. As divisive as this journey had been, we were all given a way to understand and accept what before we could not. It seems to be that everything has its price—and that includes curiosity and love. And I was fortunate in that, for me, the price for one included the other.

In January 1992, I was released from Terminal Island Federal Penitentiary to a halfway house in San Francisco; where I was to remain for six months with the remainder of my ten year sentence to be served on parole. There at the halfway house, I met Michael Savage, who was just beginning his sojourn in the federal prison system. One evening, I read Michael my poem, *The Journey and the Gypsy Girl*.

After listening, Michael said, "It's not finished, there's more."

And that night, as if on cue, six additional verses of *The Journey and the Gypsy Girl* were written.

TO THE GYPSY GIRL

It all turned out like you said it would
Medellin and Marrakech
Big Bird and the laundry job
And there's more I can't confess

But you didn't tell me of the sorrows
Of the partings and my tears
You didn't tell me of the journey
Through all my hidden fears

She smiled at me at my heartfelt words
And said she'd known that when
I'd come back in the future
That I'd still owe her the ten

That if I'd paid she'd have told me all
Of what there was to hear
But she knew back then I'd survive it all
And then she drew me near

I smelled the flowers in her hair
Her blouse lay on the floor
We kissed and laughed and did the things
That make you wish for more

And now I'm free as the Gypsy girl
And my heart is filled with love
For that which made this journey
So different from what it was

———————

EPILOGUE

Other Writings, Pre and Post Prison

THIRION'S TALE
PART II

Norman Thirion's plan to get out of prison was brilliant. The fact that it didn't work didn't mean it wasn't brilliant; it only meant it didn't work. In fact, when Norman first told me what he was about to do, I thought his plan was very good. And, it was. It was just that Thirion's plan was different than what I thought it was.

When Norman had discovered that his appeal had been turned down by the appellate court, he had taken me to his quarters, showed me some documents and asked if I would write down the story he was about to tell and keep a copy of it for safekeeping. Norman said he needed the story in the hands of a third party in order to insure his safety because of what he was about to do.

At the time, the spring of 1987, the White House and the federal prison system were very much in the control of the Reagan inner circle, the very men Thirion believed responsible for framing him and sending him to prison. A presidential election was coming up the next year in 1988 and Thirion reasoned that the last thing the Republicans wanted was a scandal linking them to the disappearance of perhaps hundreds of millions of dollars intended for the Afghan freedom fighters, a link he could easily provide if they didn't use their influence to get him an early release and pardon.

Once Thirion knew I had written down his story, he wrote a letter addressed to Otis Chandler, the owner/publisher of the Los Angeles Times. In it, Thirion referred to the times, when in the employ of Howard Hughes, he had met Chandler and his wife on different occasions. He said the purpose of his letter was that he, Thirion, could shed some light on events that had recently been reported in Chandler's L.A. Times. Events that included the discovery of a secret CIA Saudi fund meant for the Afghan resistance that Dr. Nake Kamrany of USC in the L.A. Times said never reached them.

I thought Thirion's letter was wonderful for it would soon expose the corruption of the Reagan White House for all to see. The only trouble was, although Thirion had addressed the letter to Otis Chandler, he never intended to send it to him. Instead, Thirion had enclosed a copy of the Chandler letter with a letter he had mailed to a prominent Republican lawyer with close ties to the Republican Party hierarchy—a lawyer who knew Thirion from his days with Howard Hughes and one who could immediately inform the Reagan White House of what Thirion was threatening to do. Thirion's letter to the lawyer also stated that the details of his story were now in the hands of a third party who would release the story to the press if anything unfortunate and unexpected should happen to Thirion while he was still in prison.

Thirion's letter to the Republican lawyer had an immediate effect. Shortly thereafter, Thirion received a phone call from the lawyer telling him to do nothing with the information. He told Thirion to sit tight until he came to see him, which would be soon. Thirion's plan was working.

Within a week, Norman was informed that he had a lawyer's visit and to report immediately to the visiting room. When Norman returned, he was elated. There, he said, he had met with three men— the lawyer to whom he had written the letter, and two others, both relatives of high ranking and prominent members of the Republican Party. One was related to Paul Laxalt, Ronald Reagan's presidential campaign manager in 1980 and '84, former governor of the state of Nevada, and soon to be candidate for the 1988 Republican nomination for the presidency. The other visitor was a relative of Orrin Hatch, ranking Republican senator from the state of Utah, and himself a candidate for the Republican nomination for the presidency some years later.

Norman said the meeting had gone well. He had explained to his visitors how he had fallen from grace. Once banker to Howard Hughes and now a federal inmate arrested in Monaco on trumped-up charges of accepting loan fees, Thirion recounted the story of his ill-fated involvement with Transglobal Productions and the men behind it—William Wilson, one of Reagan's closest associates, and General Robert E. Cushman, former commandant of the U.S. Marine Corps and past deputy director of the CIA, etc.

Norman told the men he believed his arrest had been engineered in order to discredit him should he ever expose the diversion of money meant for the Afghan resistance. Thirion had been cut out of a deal where he had been promised 2% of all moneys raised, which amounted to $10 million. Those in the Republican White House knew Thirion would be angry and had taken preemptive steps to discredit Thirion should he ever tell what actually had happened.

The three men who listened to Thirion's story knew exactly what could happen if the story got out. The Reagan White House was already under attack for its role in the Iran-Contra money-for-arms scandal. Now, a story that alleged the embezzlement of millions of dollars intended for the Afghan resistance could have a chilling effect on the Republican chances for the presidency the following year. The men asked Norman what he wanted. Norman replied, "I want justice." They answered, "Give us some time. We'll get you out."

Norman's plan indeed seemed to be working. I had hoped Norman's plan was to include releasing details of the Transglobal story to the Los Angeles Times but it didn't. The purpose of Norman's plan was not to enlighten the American public about the covert world of politics and money. Norman already had an intimate knowledge of the Machiavellian world of the American political process. For ten years he had worked for Howard Hughes, a man who believed that buying influence and politicians was the cheapest way of doing business.

The Marina Del Rey project in Los Angeles had been a Howard Hughes project that Thirion had financially managed. Thirion said that Hughes' partner in the deal was a group led by Herb Kalmbach, the personal attorney of Richard Nixon. It was Thirion's opinion that it was not for the financing clout or real estate expertise of Kalmbach that Hughes had included the Nixon crowd in the lucrative Marina Del Rey development. No, Norman already knew too much about the real political process and his plan didn't include exposing it. The only purpose of Norman's plan was to get Norman Thirion out of prison as soon as possible. And, being there myself, I couldn't fault him a bit.

The prison experience dashes many hopes, and Norman's was to be among them. His elation was short lived. Although his prospects for release were initially high, the calls to the lawyer and Laxalt's and Hatch's relatives were not to bring Thirion the news he hoped for. As the weeks turned into months, Thirion realized the efforts of the three men were not going to get him out of prison. Confirmation of his fears came when they told him they had informed Wilson of Thirion's plan to tell what he knew unless he was released from prison. Wilson had replied, "Let him tell. No one will believe him."

The arrogance of William Wilson's answer was to be unfortunately justified; not because no one would believe it, but because no one wanted the story told, not even Norman Thirion. Finally released from prison, Thirion later wrote me and asked me to forget the story. It was understandable. Thirion had been an international banker and had moved easily and naturally in the corridors of power, corridors where scandal is avoided like the plague because there, as in society, virtue is measured not by fact, but by reputation. Thirion had a life to rebuild and the less anyone knew of his imprisonment the better.

I, however, had no reputation to lose. I was a convicted drug dealer, a group the media vilified with the same fervor it had previously reserved for child molesters and traitors and now blamed for most of society's ills. I, however, cared little if people knew I had been in prison. Being a prisoner in a police state is, in itself, not necessarily a bad thing.

At the time, the San Francisco Chronicle had been running a series of articles written by a federal inmate and I thought the Chronicle would be interested in Norman's story. I was wrong. I sent a letter detailing what I had been told to the editors of the Chronicle but heard nothing in reply. I next thought of notifying the U.S.

Department of Justice about what I knew. But the Department of Justice was securely in the control of the Republican Party and writing them would be akin to writing Goebbels in Nazi Germany, informing him that a nice Jewish family in the neighborhood had disappeared and I believed the police were responsible. No, I thought, Norman's story would have to wait until I was released from prison.

In the summer of 1992, I was released, and although still on parole, I was now free to tell what I knew. I figured that the Democrats would be interested in my tale of Republican corruption, so I went to the offices of California's Democratic senators, Barbara Boxer and Diane Feinstein. Because I had served on Diane Feinstein's China Committee when she was the Mayor of San Francisco, I figured my chances were better with Diane. I was wrong again.

During Diane's tenure as mayor, I had been asked to give a talk to the San Francisco Port Commission on behalf of my Republican landlord and prominent local society figure, Ed Osgood. At the time, I was importing Chinese hand-knotted carpets, the import duties were 45%, and Ed's duty-free foreign trade zone was the most cost-effective place to store them until sold.

I gave the talk before the Port Commission and ended up photographed on the front page of the S.F. Chronicle business section extolling the virtues of San Francisco's China trade and the value of Ed Osgood's Foreign Trade Zone. For that, I was rewarded with a seat on Mayor Feinstein's China Committee and later accompanied Diane on a trip to Shanghai to speak before various Shanghai import-export corporations.

My previous relationship with Diane notwithstanding, my story about the Republican skim was to fall on deaf ears. I spoke with one of her aides who listened carefully to what I had to say. But during the conversation, I could sense this was a story they didn't want to know. Barbara Boxer's office, too, was solicitous but in the end declined to take any action.

I was learning a cold hard lesson in modern American politics that I had not been taught when getting my degree in political science at UC Davis years earlier; to wit, when it comes to the powerful, no one wants to point fingers. I thought because the story included politically powerful figures such as President Ronald Reagan, retired Marine General and former CIA Deputy Director Robert E. Cushman, and Ambassador William Wilson, and countries such as Saudi Arabia and Afghanistan and covert agencies such as the Central Intelligence Agency and the National Security Council, there would be a great deal of interest in the story.

I was wrong. Just the opposite is true. In America, as elsewhere in the world, everyone is afraid to accuse the powerful of wrongdoing. If the culprit had been a poor black women selling crack to fund a black women's uprising, the outcry would have been deafening. As it was, I couldn't get a response.

Whether it was my stubbornness or stupidity, I continued intermittently to attempt to tell the story fate had so ungraciously given me. The next attempt was inspired by the vitriolic Republican attacks on the Democratic administration of Bill Clinton. Surely, they could use some ammunition to defend themselves against the relentless rage of the Republicans.

Again, I was to be wrong. In the fall of 1994, I contacted Webster Hubbell, Clinton's beleaguered associate and offered to send him what I knew. Hubbell, at least initially, was both eager and grateful, thanking me for the information and promising it would get into the right hands. If the information did, I was never to know. Hubbell's thank you was the last thing I was to hear from him.

My attempts to tell Thirion's story of Republican malfeasance grew fewer as the combination of repeated rebuffs and passing years convinced me that no one wanted to know. Only three more times would a spark of unfounded optimism cause me to once again send Norman's tale out in the vain hope that someone, somewhere out there would care enough to investigate.

Information was sent to Bob Woodward of the Washington Post, Bill Kurtis of A&E's Investigative Reports, and to the investigative reporters at the Los Angeles Times. If they didn't care enough to investigate, then no one would. No one did.

The burden of hearing a tale as extraordinary as Thirion's and realizing that no one wants to hear it has not been an easy one to bear. Carrying this story around since 1987 has been a bitter task and the lack of feedback and support has only fueled my cynical view of America and American politics and the American media.

Alexis De Toqueville predicted in 1835 in his extraordinary book, *Democracy In America*, that (1) the United States and Russia would someday represent opposing views on the world stage, (2) the United States could become a police state where the people lost the political will to govern themselves, and (3) the rebirth of freedom in America would come through the arts. Only De Toqueville's third prediction hasn't come true, the rebirth of freedom in America has yet to occur.

In an ironic footnote to Norman's story, in June 2001, I wondered what had happened to Norman Thirion. My curiosity caused me to enter his name, Norman Bernard Thirion, into Google, the internet search engine. Because I had been disappointed so often in the past, I didn't expect anything different this time. But this time I was to be wrong. This time another piece in the story told by Norman Thirion was to fall unexpectedly into place.

There, on my computer screen, the words, Norman Bernard Thirion, had taken me to the site of Georgetown University's Lauinger Library's special collection of Ambassador William A. Wilson's papers spanning the years 1980-1992.

There, in box 1, folder 54, was noted the following correspondence, "@ Roger W. Hunt, Hunt & Haugaard, attorneys at law, South Dakota. Includes correspondence from the following re the invasion of Afghanistan by the USSR: Norman Bernard Thirion, International Banking Services to W.A.W. (William A. Wilson). General Abdul Wali to W.A.W., copy, E.T. Barwick, E.T. Barwick Industries, Inc., Georgia, to Prince Bandar Ibn Sultan, copy*."

Just as fate had unexpectedly given me Norman's story fifteen years before, fate, now, just as unexpectedly had corroborated Norman's story regarding his relationship with Reagan's alleged bagman, Ambassador William A. Wilson. The names in Wilson's file were familiar to me, told to me by Thirion years before—Roger Hunt was Norman's attorney and had handled his appeal, General Abdul Wali had been the aide to the former King of Afghanistan, Zahir Shah, who headed the Afghan resistance that was to receive the Saudi money; E.T. Barwick of Atlanta, Georgia, was Thirion's partner, and Prince Bandar Ibn Sultan received the proposal to fund the Afghan Government-In-Exile on behalf of the Saudi royal family.

William Wilson's gift to Georgetown University revealed further evidence of Wilson's participation. In box 2, folder 56 of Wilson's bequest to Georgetown University, were papers sent by USC Professor Dr. Nake Kamrany to William Wilson and to Saudi Prince Bandar Bin Sultan regarding Afghanistan's independence from the USSR.

Because Dr. Kamrany had been a central figure in the events recounted by Norman Thirion, I had always been curious about what Dr. Kamrany actually knew. So, two years after Google had unexpectedly provided proof of William Wilson's participation, I decided in May 2004 to contact Dr. Kamrany directly.

I e-mailed Dr. Kamrany at the University of Southern California. I said I possessed information provided by Norman Thirion regarding a possible skim of Saudi funds intended for the Afghan resistance. My e-mail got an immediate response. Dr. Kamrany called back and launched into an emphatic denial of Thirion's assertions.

He asked how I knew Norman and how I got my information. I told Kamrany I had met Norman in prison and was writing a book about my experiences. Kamrany then confirmed he knew Norman Thirion, William Wilson, Perry Morgan, and General Cushman. He did deny, however, any knowledge of Transglobal Productions or about a conspiracy to skim the funds. He did say that General Cushman had mentioned a private venture.

Kamrany also denied knowing Transglobal directors Dr. Jon Speller and Rabbi Morton Rosenthal (Rabbi Rosenthal was the Transglobal director who played a key role in the purchase of captured Soviet Syrian arms from Israel). Kamrany did admit he had seen the Soviet armaments used by the Afghan resistance in Afghanistan and personally had never received an adequate explanation about where the large supply of Soviet arms had come from.

Then Kamrany unexpectedly asked if I knew anyone in the movie business (I was to find out his son had an idea for a movie). It was a question that was to lead to our meeting in person. Rawson Marshall Thurber, my friend Marshall's son, had recently written and directed a movie that was about to be released. The movie, Dodgeball, was opening nationwide June 18th and Marshall had invited friends and family to a private showing in Los Angeles on the 17th. I obtained invitations from Marshall for Dr. Kamrany and his guests to attend.

There, I met Dr. Kamrany and we continued our discussion. After our talk, I had no doubt what Norman had told me was the truth, that Kamrany's denial of a skim was based only upon his ignorance of its existence. The conversation confirmed that Kamrany had absolutely no knowledge of Transglobal Productions or any inkling of the conspiratorial designs of its principals.

Finally, now, after the revelations of the internet and my meeting with Dr. Kamrany, I was to get some closure to the extraordinary story I had heard during my first year in prison. And with it came a realization that has given me a measure of acceptance and peace: Two thousand years ago, the Pharisees and Publicans were in power. They still are today. A story isn't going to change anything.

There is, however, an interesting detail that still remains unresolved. When I entered Norman Bernard Thirion into Google's search engine, I also googled the names of others alleged to have participated in the skim. Transglobal director, Rabbi Morton Rosenthal and Transglobal vice-president Dr. Jon Speller in particular brought up interesting information.

When I googled the name of Dr. Jon Speller, a website connected Dr. Speller not only to Rabbi Rosenthal, but also to a company "Transglobal Resources" co-owned by the two men.

The weblink stated:

"The key link between the ADL [Anti Defamation League] *and the Sikh extremists who murdered Prime Minister Gandhi runs through Rabbi Rosenthal a senior ADL employee and head of the league's Latin American Affairs Division, who is directly linked to the man who ordered the assassination, Dr. Jagjit Singh Chauhan. It also runs through Rosenthal's longtime intimate political collaborator and sometimes business partner Jon Speller. Speller is widely believed to be a high-level intelligence agent for British intelligence* [with] *documented links to Israeli, Soviet, and American intelligence services. One year before Mrs. Gandhi's assassination, Speller sponsored a U.S. visit by Jagjit Singh Chauhan...After Mrs. Gandhi's death, Rabbi Rosenthal and Speller, operating through a front company they had jointly established called Transglobal Resources, arranged a series of secret meetings in Washington, London, and Quito, Ecuador, which resulted in the Ecuadoran government offering Chauhan a large tract of land on which to establish a Khalistani homeland."*

But, by far the most interesting link occurred when I entered the name Ronald Sablosky into Google's search engine. When Norman Thirion was fired as Transglobal's banker, General Cushman replaced Thirion with Ronald Sablosky; and, in 2002, a search on the internet was to connect Ronald Sablosky directly to the office of President Ronald Reagan.

The name Ronald Sablosky led to a Google first page reference to the site of the Presidential Papers of the Ronald Reagan Library. There, in Box 92335 of the litigation files of Jonathan Scharfen, legal advisor to the National Security Council under President Reagan, was the case US v. Ronald Sablosky.

Advised by the Reagan Library to submit a Freedom of Information Act request to review the White House file, I did so in August 2002. I was informed it would take 22-24 months to process the request which included a 30-day notification to the representatives of President Reagan and current President George W. Bush. After processing, remaining national security information would be sent to appropriate agencies for classification review. I was told it may take more than a year for the agencies to notify the Library of their recommendations.

In April 2006, 44 months after the FOIA request was submitted, I have yet to receive the information requested; yet, two interesting changes have occurred. First, googling the name Ronald Sablosky no longer brings up the prominent reference to US v. Sablosky as it did in 2002. Secondly, by cross referencing "reagan" and "scharfen" on Google, I did again locate the case US v. Sablosky, now with the words "farm loan scheme" prominently in parentheses next to it.

What I find curious is that loan fees allegedly charged to farmers was the basis of the indictment used by the federal government to prosecute Norman Thirion in 1984, charges Norman maintained were patently false and designed solely to discredit what Thirion might divulge about the Reagan White House. Did Ronald Sablosky also run afoul of his White House masters, thereby causing National Security Council lawyers to fabricate and institute similar litigation against him?

Perhaps there are other reasons why Jonathan Scharfen, counsel for the powerful National Security Council under President Reagan, would file charges against a Ronald Sablosky regarding a "farm loan scheme". Perhaps it's not the same Ronald Sablosky chosen by former CIA Deputy Director and retired Marine Commandant General Robert E. Cushman to negotiate the transfer of the Saudi funds. Perhaps.

Irrespective of what the files eventually do reveal, I am now confident the story confided to me by Norman Thirion is true. I am also confident those in the Reagan inner circle who skimmed the Saudi funds of perhaps hundreds of millions of dollars will never be brought to justice. For other than to preserve the common order, the majority of civil and criminal laws are written to protect the powerful, not to prosecute them.

Quis Custodiat Custodes? The Latin saying is as true today as it was in ancient Rome. Who Will Guard The Guardians? Certainly not you, certainly not I, and certainly not the courts and the U.S. criminal justice system.

Imperial Rome, Imperial America. In the past, some historians have blamed the decline of the Roman Empire on the decadence of its citizenry. If, however, the present is in any way a reflection of the past, it is far more likely it was a combination of corruption and greed that paved Rome's well-greased path to entropy and decline.

May romp and happenstance someday
Replace pomp and circumstance

PROSPECTS FOR THE FUTURE

I have recently come across the amazing story of Catherine Austin Fitts. In 1987, at the same time Norman Thirion was telling me his story of Republican malfeasance, Catherine Austin Fitts was Managing Director at Dillon, Read & Co. Inc., a most Republican and major Wall Street investment house. Fitts was to later serve as Assistant Secretary of Housing at HUD in the Republican administration of President George Bush, Sr.

Fitts' insider story, *Dillon, Read & Co. Inc. & The Aristocracy of Prison Profits*, is a must-read for all who wish to understand why and how the United States of America has become the world's number one jailor, imprisoning a higher percentage of its citizens than any country in the world.

First serialized at www.narconews.com/Issue40/article1644.html, and now available at www.dunwalke.com, Catherine Austin Fitts' rare and revealing insider story chronicles the events by which Republicans and Democrats alike now profit at the trough of the misnamed "War On Drugs", an ongoing and highly lucrative operation run from Washington DC for the benefit of Wall Street investors and tenured DC politicians with profits generated by sending increasingly greater numbers of Americans to jail.

Begun by the Republicans, the "War on Drugs" rapidly accelerated under the Democratic administration of Bill Clinton and Al Gore. During Clinton and Gore's term, the US prison population "coincidentally" doubled at the same time the Democrats successfully lobbied the US Department of Justice to begin sending its prisoners to private prisons. Catherine Austin Fitts' story is a fascinating tale of how powerful business and political interests conspire to divert government generated funds to their own pockets via the so-called "privatization" of government services.

The privatization of healthcare, criminal justice, and military services, etc., creates extraordinary opportunities for corporations and well-connected individuals of both parties to obscenely profit from public moneys and public policy. While the Republican Party proclaims its opposition to big government, it is Republicans who primarily benefit by the privatization of government's bloated budgets. And, now, Democrats, under Clinton and Gore, have discovered they, too, can play the same game.

Privatization, born on the watch of President Reagan, grew during the administration of President George Bush Sr. where Dick Cheney, Secretary of Defense, commissioned a study on the outsourcing of military expenditures. It then gained momentum under Bill Clinton and now has reached adulthood in President George W. Bush and Vice-President Dick Cheney's administration of America's needs and priorities.

Catherine Austin Fitts observes:
What people miss is the extent to which...this intentional centralism is deeply pervasive and therefore deeply bipartisan. It receives the promotion and support from all political and social spectrums that make money by running government through the contractors, banks,

law firms, think tanks and universities that really run the government. My intention for this story is to make clear how the system really works. A system in which a small group of ambitious insiders who more often than not were educated at Harvard, Yale, Princeton, and other Ivy League schools enjoy centralizing power and advantaging themselves. Paradigms of Republican vs. Democrat or Conservative vs. Progressive have been designed for obfuscation and entertainment.

The collusion of Republicans and Democrats to enrich themselves by conspiring against the public good also coincides with the loss of America's civil liberties on an unprecedented scale, the breakdown of the constitutional separation between church and state, a takeover of the Supreme Court by extreme right wing judicial activists, the control of the White House, Congress, and media by powerful corporate and special interests, and a voting process so prone to fraud it cannot be certified by international observers. Not since the earliest days of the republic has the well-being of America been so at risk.

These are indeed dark days for America. I believe, however, this is cause for optimism. If it is darkest before the dawn, the New Age cannot be too far away.

LAISSEZ LE BON TEMPS ROULEZ!

If you seek to understand the world of human activity
look first to the self-interests of those involved
As true for the whole as it is for the parts
you will by so doing come to understand the actions
of nations as well as the behavior
of individual men and women
And when you do discover what the underlying self-interests are
you will discover too
the actual nature of the self then being served

DEMOCRACY IN AMERICA REDUX

"Is this what American democracy is producing? Men and women who, just below the surface, are barbarians?"
Cardinal James Stafford, 2005

As much as American torture in Iraq has surprised the world, it probably would not have surprised Alexis DeToqueville, author of ***Democracy in America***. Written in 1835 and still required reading in most American history courses, DeToqueville's ***Democracy in America*** is rarely understood as being both an observation <u>and</u> critique of America's experiment with popular rule.

DeToqueville saw democracy in America as flawed—an impossible marriage between two conflicting desires: the desire to be led and the desire to be free. DeToqueville pointed out that Americans, having placed their freedoms in the hands of a central authority, believed themselves free because the central authority was of their own choosing. To DeToqueville, however, that Americans elected their master did not make them free. It only meant they chose their master.

DeToqueville believed a nation where citizens abdicate responsibility for governance except for the election of their masters would result in a corrupt and dehumanized society. Of such an experiment, DeToqueville wrote:

> *It is in vain to summon a people, who have been rendered so dependent on the central power to choose from time to time the representatives of that power;* <u>*this rare and brief exercise of their free choice, however important it may be, will not prevent them from gradually losing the faculties of thinking, feeling, and acting for themselves, and thus gradually falling below the level of humanity.*</u>

With these prescient words, DeToqueville predicted in 1835 the America we see today—a nation governed by leaders who invite and excuse torture, promote fear and war, and use the police powers of the state to benefit the wealthy at the expense of the poor. All this with a democratic electorate evenly divided on whether this is good or bad. DeToqueville would not have been surprised.

As always, the choice is to be led or to be free. Leaders say you can have it both ways. Experience teaches otherwise.

The opposite of order is not anarchy
The opposite of order and anarchy
Is harmony

TRUE GOVERNANCE / SELF-GOVERNANCE
By
Dee Hock

True governance is based on understanding that even simple societies are far too complex to expect that there can be agreement in the particular. Systems of self-governance, in the individual and at every scale beyond, are based on understanding that ordinances, orders, and enforcement deal with an absence of true governance. They are an attempt to compel the kind of behavior that organizations fail to induce. Ordinances, orders, and enforcement are simply different words for control, command, and tyranny. This ultimate sanction of control is force. Force is the root of tyranny. Those who rise in a tyrannical world are those least capable of self-governance or inducement of it in others, else they would not engage in tyranny. And when they rise, it is axiomatic that self-governance will decline and government will gradually be for the benefit of the few and not the many. It will inexorably become destructive. Ultimately, there will be no limit to that destruction, for there appears to be no limit to the ability of the rational mind to create devices to alter and manipulate all life forms and all aspects of the physical world.

GOVERNMENT

"Samos, my dear friend, how are you?"

"Well, Atmos, very well. In fact, I have just discovered a most amazing device."

"A new device?"

"Yes. It's called a government."

"A government? Pray, what does it do?"

"It takes care of everything, Atmos. It keeps order in the kingdom and dispenses justice. It does whatever needs to be done."

"Indeed. And what is its price?"

"I need only feed it, and even in that it is most efficient. It tells me exactly how much it needs in order to accomplish my goals and, in doing so, it takes nothing for itself."

"Really? It does sound rather extraordinary."

"I myself am quite satisfied with it. For having no goals of its own, it exists only to serve what needs to be done."

"A truly selfless device, Samos, if indeed it is. Have you no complaints?"

"Not really. Although of late its appetite seems to have grown tremendously. But, then again, it is because my needs have grown."

"Your needs have grown, Samos? You were doing quite well when I saw you last. How do you know this to be true?"

"It has told me so, Atmos. Day and night, it monitors my kingdom watching over the welfare of my people, and telling me what needs to be accomplished and how to go about it. I am fortunate to have discovered it. I now can finally have some rest."

"You actually discovered it?"

"Not exactly. Rather it offered me its services. It said if I wasn't satisfied, I could always change it."

"Some guarantee, my friend."

"Yes. I thought so myself."

Atmos was quiet for a long time. When he next spoke, his brow was furrowed and his voice serious.

"Samos, my dear friend, the cost of your rest may be higher than you think. I have heard of these devices on other planes though there they are known by other names. Beware, Samos, beware. Little as yet is known of these devices but their early promise seems to be never kept and I doubt if your experience will be different."

"They have these devices on other planes?"

"They do."

"And what is it they say of it, dear Atmos?"

"They say it begins as your guardian but soon becomes your guard."

"So there is danger..."

"So it would seem."

"And when does the danger begin?"

"When you listen to its words."

"Then it may be too late."

"It may be, my friend. It may be."

CANTERBURY TALES REDUX
THE TRAVELER'S TALE

A tale to tell that you might hear
The truth of all of that we fear
That and which we hope to be
That and which we'll never see
A tale so old that it might be
Greece or Rome or Brittany
A tale of power you would know
Except you still deny it so

For once again we've gone astray
And once again we'll rue the day
By standing not for what is true
By standing not for what we knew
But let us now this tale be told
A tale new yet a tale old

The traveler spoke to us that day
Of a kingdom far away
He said the kingdom although young
Was watched by all in Christendom

For it was hoped that it would be
A beacon for the world to see

A light of justice a torch for peace
Opportunity within reach
How might this be a voice did ask
When such has never come to pass
That ever since man ruled man
The rule has been by iron hand

The traveler said it was to be
Ruled in ways quite differently
There was to be no king or queen
Nor any manner where it would seem
That one was better than the rest
It was to be a noble quest

It was to be a kingdom fair
Where all would be an equal there
Where every one would have a voice
Where everyone would have a choice
Those who governed would the people serve
Not themselves but those deserved

Such a kingdom it was to be
A kingdom where all would see
That man could rule not selfishly
But for the good of all and could then be
An example fair just and wise
No longer then would man devise
Ways to enslave his fellow man
Because he could because he can

When the traveler spoke as he did, a quiet fell over us, his fellow pilgrims. Not only was the traveler's tale markedly different than of the miller, the knight, and the sea captain, the traveler's tale had made us all uneasy. As if by listening we were somehow complicit in approving of this new kingdom's revolutionary way of government. We all knew to even talk of popular rule was seditious and if the King's spies were about, who knew what manner of trouble could greet us at Canterbury.

We thought perhaps the innkeeper might stop the traveler from continuing, for it was the innkeeper who had devised the telling of tales to pass the time to and from Canterbury. But when the innkeeper spoke, it was to question the traveler, not to admonish him.

"Quite a tale, dear traveler, and when, pray tell, did this occur?"

"In the future, dear innkeeper" replied the traveler. "The events of which I speak are still yet to be."

"And the new kingdom of which you speak, where is its location?"

"In a land called America," answered the traveler. "It is a land still yet to be discovered."

"Since your story happens in the future and in a land still yet to be discovered" said the innkeeper, "then I see no reason not to continue. For such a story is purely of the imagination, and there can be no harm in either the telling or hearing of such."

The innkeeper looked around to see if any would think otherwise and when no one voiced an objection, he bade the traveler continue with his unusual tale.

"How did this new nation come to be?"

"The nation's birth was by revolution, by waging a war of independence against the greatest empire the world had then known."

"Greater than Alexander's or that of Rome?" a fellow pilgrim asked.

"Yes, the empire was so great it will be said the sun never set upon it."

"Yet, pray tell, you say this nation wrested its independence from such a great empire?

"Yes" the traveler continued, "And its war of independence was only exceeded by its declaration of independence, a declaration which stated all men were created equal and were entitled to life, liberty, and the pursuit of justice."

"Hear, hear!" approving voices cried out. Obviously, the traveler's tale had so captured the imagination of his fellow pilgrims that they had lost all fear of the King's spies.

"Did this nation's declaration of independence and the rights of man then cause an uprising of all nations and all peoples against all tyrannies and the yoke of empire?"

"No" answered the traveler, "It did, however, light a flame of hope that such might someday be so. While the rest of the great land known as America still lay in subjugation, the very name America became identified with this new nation and the desire and pursuit of freedom and liberty for all mankind.

"Hear, hear!" more cheers did ring out at such news.

The traveler's tale had obviously captured the imagination of all who journeyed to Canterbury. The story of a new land called America, with its dreams of freedom, did inspire us to know more about this new nation. That is, until, the next question was asked.

"This great empire against which this nation rebelled, what was its name?"

"England."

A gasp of surprise arose. We were shocked at the traveler's unexpected answer.

"England, hear, hear." A cry rang out and we all in joined to celebrate the discovery that our very own England was to be the greatest empire the world had ever known.

"England, then, is to be the very empire upon which the sun does not set?"

"Yes, that is so."

More cheering greeted the traveler's revelation. I, however, could not but remember that only moments before we had been cheering the birth of the nation that had successfully revolted against England's apparently tyrannical rule.

As the cheers continued, the crowd began to question the traveler.

"How many countries did England rule?"

"By what means did England achieve its empire, by its navy or its army?"

It was now obvious our desire was to learn about the greatness of England's empire, not mankind's quest for freedom and liberty. Then a voice asked,

"What happened to England's empire when America rebelled against its rule?"

The pilgrims quieted at the question, anxiously awaiting the answer.

"Nothing" said the traveler, "Nothing at all. Except for the loss of its American colonies, England's empire continued to expand well into the next century even after America's successful rebellion."

"Hear, hear."

"Long live the King!"

Cheers again erupted at the news of England's continued greatness.

"Into the next century? And what century might that be?" someone asked.

"The nineteenth century," the traveler answered, "England's empire will begin in the seventeenth century and will reach its peak in the nineteenth century, in the year 1850."

We were stunned. England, our very own England was to rule an empire on which the sun was to never set and England's empire was to reach its peak in 1850; almost five hundred years hence, the present year being but 1385.

My fellow pilgrims, however, seemed to be adversely affected by the news England's great empire was still a ways off, a few hundred years at least. Too far in the future for any now present to reap any personal benefit. The parson could not count on gifts to build the new parsonage nor could the knight see immediate opportunity for more glory, nor the miller increased revenues as a result of England's future empire. Such hopes now dimmed, the pilgrims' attention turned back to what the traveler was to say next.

"England's power and wealth in 1850 is to be unrivaled. Its coin is to be the basis of world trade and its fleet of ships would bring wealth from its many colonies back to its shores. But one hundred years later, in 1950, America will have replaced England as the most powerful and wealthy kingdom in all Christendom."

"Will England be displaced as the result of war?" a pilgrim asked.

"War will play but a minor role in England's decline," the traveler answered. "England's demise will come not as a result of war, but from the cost of empire. In 1870, England will begin to import more goods than it exports. At the same time its military budget will grow so large that by the end of the century, England's treasury, once the world's richest will be no longer so. A costly war in the beginning of the 1900s will then leave England but a shadow of its former self."

"And by 1950, America, like England one century before, will be the world's most powerful nation. Like England previous, its coin will be the basis of world trade and at mid century America will possess three quarters of the world's monetary gold, an amount so great that no nation previous had ever possessed so large a sum."

A pilgrim asked, "Will America's empire be greater than that of England?"

"America, almost wealthy beyond measure in 1950, will possess no empire."

All of us were unprepared for this answer and we listened as he continued. "Unlike all previous nations of wealth, nations such as England, Spain, Portugal, and Rome, America will not come by its wealth by empire. America will come by its wealth by industry and circumstance."

"Pray tell, what manner of circumstance, dear traveler, brought America its wealth?"

"Abundant land, the fortune of providence, and two great wars fought on the land of others which left America untouched and wealthy and the rest of the world devastated and in debt."

We who listened to the traveler's tale were amazed at this strange tale of America's great fortune. Unique among nations, champion of liberty and freedom, wealthy not by plunder and empire, America seemed indeed blessed by providence.

"How long, then, is to America reign as the wealthiest of all nations?"

"Not long. Within twenty short years, by 1970, America will overspend its entire hoard of gold."

A murmur could be heard from all who listened.

"In twenty years?"

"The hoard of gold America possesses in 1950 will disappear in but twenty years?"

"How can this be?" someone asked. "Did America buy so much more than it sold?"

"No," the traveler answered. "During those twenty years, its exports will far exceed its imports, though like England one century before, this would soon change."

"By what manner, then, will America spend its wealth?"

"America will spend its wealth in pursuit of empire."

A voice cried out, asking for all of us one question.

"If America needed no empire for wealth, why would it spend all its gold in pursuit of empire?"

"Because America had no need of empire, did not mean America will not yearn for empire. Finding itself alone among nations in wealth and power in 1950, America desired to extend its military, political, and economic dominion over the world. To this end, it will send so much capital abroad that by 1970, it will owe more than it possesses and to keep what gold it will have, America will then refuse to pay the gold it owes, paying others only with printed money."

"If America could not pay its debts, then its reign as the world's greatest power must have also ended?"

"In the past," the traveler answered, "that would have been so, but America's power and might is to be so great, all nations, caught off guard by America's bankruptcy will accept America's printed money without requiring gold to make up what was owing. This will allow America to print ever more until its profligate spending will endanger the entire world."

"Are the hopes and dreams represented by America never to be?" a voice cried out, "What is to become of America?"

"The hopes and dreams of mankind will live on regardless of whether any nation embodies those ideals. As to what happens to America, you will hear the answer upon our return from Canterbury. You will also find out what happens when America—with England, Spain, and Portugal, all former great colonial empires at its side— declares war on another nation to secure for itself that nation's rich natural resources."

"Once David, now Goliath, America will find itself increasingly alone, pursuing empire in a world needing vision and cooperation. What America then chooses to do will determine its place in the history of nations."

Now, my friends, let us continue on our journey. Godspeed.

GOLD, MONEY, POWER AND 9/11
With the rise of central banking, gold as money began a three century decline. Gold as power, however, continued on as usual.

In 1971, when the US cut the ties between money and gold, gold as money ceased to exist. Gold as power, however, continued. But because gold is power there is little real information on the connection between the two; and that information is often misleading as the powerful prefer secrecy and the true movements of gold are no exception.

I would like to share some information I discovered about the world of gold and power that will shed light on some very critical issues; and, because of power's purposefully hidden path, the truth here can only be approached obliquely.

What I offer is a name. The name is Bruce Rappaport. Twenty-five years ago, in extenuating circumstances I had met Howard Hughes' private banker, Dr. Norman Bernard Thirion. Prior to working for Hughes, Dr. Thirion had worked for Daniel K. Ludwig, a man even wealthier and more secretive than Hughes.

Because of the unique circumstances under which we met, Thirion told me about events he had told few others, events that led to, among others, the name of Bruce Rappaport. The events centered on the embezzlement by the Reagan White House of funds Thirion had solicited from the Saudi royal family.

The funds, $500 million, intended to aid the Afghan freedom fighters never reached them. Instead they were later discovered in a secret CIA Swiss bank account co-mingled with proceeds from the Iran-Contra arms scandal, another illegal Reagan operation. The bank account was controlled by an Israeli-Swiss banker, Bruce Rappaport, later connected to the events surrounding 9/11.

It was because of what Howard Hughes' private banker told me in 1987 that I recognized Rappaport's name when it came to my attention last year in 2011, this time in connection with 9/11 and events far from Norman Thirion and the Reagan White House; events that will reveal the continuing connection between gold, money and power.

SECRET LIES AND HIDDEN TRUTHS

The name of Bruce Rappaport brings together events, nations and individuals tangled in interlocking webs of deceit and deception. The covert life of Bruce Rappaport is similar to a USB hub that connects crime, power, politics and money; and it was Rappaport's relationship with William Casey (Nixon's Chairman of the SEC, Reagan's Director of the CIA and Rappaport's golfing buddy) that gave Rappaport his greased entry into the international sewers of power and money.

On August 22, 1999, an article in the New York Times, *Russian Money-Laundering Investigation finds a Familiar Swiss Banker in the Middle*, focused on Russian money-laundering then being carried out at Rappaport's bank, the Bank of New York.

The New York Times' article on Bruce Rappaport, i.e. the 'familiar Swiss banker', and his bank, the Bank of New York, did not, however, mention Rappaport's close ties to Israel, the Reagan administration and to US intelligence.

Regarding these omissions by the New York Times, Robert Parry wrote: *...the article sketched Rappaport's biography from his birth in Haifa, now part of Israel, through his founding of Inter-Maritime Bank in Geneva to his acquisition of the Bank of New York.*

But left out was an important piece of the mystery: Rappaport's close relationship to Israel's Labor Party, the Reagan administration and U.S. intelligence... Rappaport had been linked to some of the Reagan administration's most controversial actions...These included: the Iran-contra affair; an Israeli bribery case that involved a U.S.-backed oil pipeline in Iraq; the scandal over the Bank of Credit and Commerce International; a curious shipment of weapons through a melon farm in Antigua to Colombian cocaine kingpins; and the October Surprise mystery, the allegations that the 1980 Reagan campaign sabotaged Carter's negotiations to free 52 American hostages held in Iran.

WHAT YOU DON'T KNOW EXPLAINS WHAT YOU DON'T UNDERSTAND

On September 24, 2011, the name, Bruce Rappaport, was mentioned on the website Veterans Today. Bruce Rappaport and Lee Wanta, a former US intelligence operative, who, like Rappaport, was involved with Reagan's illegal Iran-contra activities, had also been active in US covert efforts to destabilize the Russian economy.

Wanta's story along with Bruce Rappaport's offers a telling glimpse into the secretive world of power, politics, money and gold. The story in Veterans Today, titled "Classified: The Wanta Chronicles, the Covert Economic War" connects Lee Wanta and Bruce Rappaport to:

.. a vast international criminal conspiracy at the heart of the American government ... [beginning] *with the criminal prosecution of former Reagan intelligence coordinator, Lee Wanta...Charges allege that the 9/11 attacks were planned and executed in order to cover financial crimes.*

The financial crimes and events that revolved around US efforts to destabilize the Russian ruble are myriad and complex; and include far more than the activities of Rappaport and Wanta.

They not only explain the events surrounding 9/11, they also reveal the source of funding for America's covert activities after WWII, thousands of tons of gold stolen from China by the Japanese—and later again stolen by the US.

CHINA'S STOLEN GOLD

Professor Chalmers Johnson's review of *Gold Warriors: America's Secret Recovery of Yamashita's Gold* by Sterling and Peggy Seagrave tells of the widespread looting of China's riches by Japanese forces before their defeat in WWII.

"Yamashita's gold" describes the vast wealth looted from China then hidden by General Yamashita. Countless tons of gold, precious stones and stolen treasures were secretly buried by General Yamashita in the Philippines prior to Japan's surrender. Ferdinand Marcos, later president of the Philippines, also had found "Yamashita's gold".

The Americans moved quickly to suppress any knowledge of this vast hoard of gold; and, rather than returning it to its rightful owners, Chalmers Johnson writes, ... *it was decided at the highest levels, presumably by Truman, to keep these discoveries secret and to funnel the money into various off-the-books slush funds to finance the clandestine activities of the CIA.*

Among these clandestine activities was the destabilization of Russia's ruble in which Rappaport and Wanta were involved, in which $240 billion of 10-year securities were issued on September

10, 1991 to buy up Russia's industrial base; and it was to destroy evidence of these covert securities and their source that the World Trade Center and the Pentagon were attacked on September 11, 2001.

According to Veterans Today, the primary targets on 9/11 in the World Trade Center were Cantor Fitzgerald and Eurobrokers, major dealers in US securities. The primary target at the Pentagon was the Office of Naval Intelligence which had been investigating the covert securities.

41% of the fatalities in the Twin Towers came from two companies that managed U.S. government securities: Cantor Fitzgerald and Eurobrokers. 31% of the 125 fatalities in the Pentagon were from the Naval Command Center that housed the Office of Naval Intelligence.

... The covert securities, used to accomplish the original national security objective had ended up in the vaults of the brokers in the World Trade Center, **[and]** *were destroyed on September 11, 2001, the day before they came due for settlement and clearing.* [bold, mine]

THE COVERUP

The Veterans Today article notes: *The federal agency mostly involved in investigating those transactions was the Office of Naval Intelligence. On September 11 those same three organizations: the two largest government securities brokers and the Office of Naval Intelligence in the US took near direct hits.*

What happened inside the buildings of the World Trade on September 11 is difficult, but not impossible to discern. The government has put a seal on the testimony gathered by the investigating 911 Commission, and instructed government employees to not speak on the matter or suffer severe penalties, but there are a number of personal testimonies posted on the internet as to what happened in those buildings that day.

Careful reconstruction from those testimonies indicates the deliberate destruction of evidence not only by a targeted assault on the buildings, but also by targeted fires and explosions. In the event that either the hijacking failed, or the buildings were not brought down, the evidence would be destroyed by fires.

Even more revealing would be the actions of the Federal Reserve Bank and the Securities and Exchange Commission on that day, and in the immediate aftermath. As one of many coincidences on September 11, the Federal Reserve Bank was operating its information system from its remote back-up site rather than its downtown headquarters.

The SEC and Federal Reserve system remained unfazed by the attack on September 11. All of their systems continued to operate. The two major security trading firms had their trade data backed up on remote systems.

Nevertheless, the Commission <u>for the first time</u> invoked its emergency powers under Securities Exchange Act Section 12(k) and issued several orders to ease certain regulatory restrictions temporarily.

On the first day of the crisis, the SEC lifted "Rule 15c3-3 -Customer Protection–Reserves and Custody of Securities," which set trading rules for certain processes. Simply, GSCC [Government Securities Clearing Corporation] *was allowed to substitute securities for the physical securities destroyed during the attack.*

Subsequent to that ruling, the GSCC issued another memo expanding blind broker settlements. A "blind broker" is a mechanism for inter-dealer transactions that maintains the anonymity of both parties to the trade. The broker serves as the agent to the principals' transactions.

<u>Thus the Federal Reserve and its GSCC had created a settlement environment totally void of controls and reporting – where it could substitute valid, new government securities for the mature, illegal securities, and not have to record where the bad securities came</u>

from, or where the new securities went – all because the paper for the primary brokers for US securities had been eliminated.

This act, alone, however was inadequate to resolve the problem, because the Federal Reserve did not have enough "takers" of the new 10 year notes. Rather than simply having to match buy and sell orders, which was the essence of resolving the "fail" problem [fails occur when securities are not delivered and paid for on the date scheduled by the buyer and seller], it appears the Fed was doing more than just matching and balancing – it was pushing new notes on the market with a special auction.

Settlement Fails in U.S. Treasury Securities

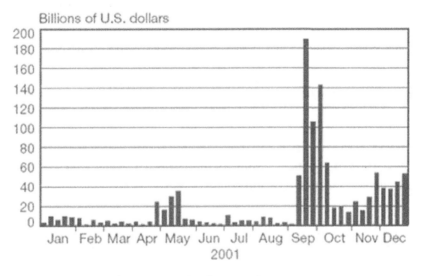

Source: Federal Reserve Bank of New York.

Note: The chart plots daily average settlement fails to deliver of U.S. Treasury securities as reported by the primary dealers for the weeks ending January 3 through December 26, 2001.

If the Federal Reserve had to cover up the clearance of $240 Billion in covert securities, they could not let the volume of capital shrink by that much in the time of a monetary crisis.

They would have had to push excess liquidity into the market, and then phase it out for a soft landing, which is exactly what appears to have happened. In about two months, the money supply was back to where it was prior to 9/11.

It was the rapid rotation of the securities settlement fails in the aftermath of September 11th that appears to have allowed the Bank of New York and the Federal Reserve to engage in a securities refinancing that resulted in the American taxpayer refinancing the $240 billion originally used for the Great Ruble Scam.

The reports published by the Federal Reserve argue that the Federal Reserve's actions increasing the monetary supply by over $300 billion were justified to overcome operational difficulties in the financial sector.

What appears to be the case is that the Federal Reserve imbalances reported on three consecutive days in the aftermath were largely concentrated at the Bank of New York, which is reported to represent over 90% of the imbalance, suggesting the Bank had been the recipient of massive fund transfers, and unable to send out transfers. This supposedly was due to major communication and system failures. **In fact, none of the Bank of New York's systems failed or went non-operational.**

The Bank of New York's suspicious actions after 9/11 were noted by The Wall Street Journal: "There is every reason to believe activities in the Bank of New York in the aftermath of September 11th are worthy of suspicion..... At one point during the week after September 11, the Bank of New York publicly reported to be overdue on $100 billion in payments."

Fedwire Funds Transfer Value and Volume,
and Aggregate Opening Balances with the
Federal Reserve: September 10-21, 2001

Date	Volume	Value (Billions of Dollars)	Balance (Billions of Dollars)
September 10	436,312	1,591	13
September 11	249,472	1,216	13
September 12	332,433	1,696	44
September 13	376,937	1,952	104 ◁
September 14	423,256	2,009	121 ◁
September 17	462,522	2,312	111 ◁
September 18	419,126	1,978	46
September 19	401,420	1,836	19
September 20	433,771	1,921	15
September 21	442,293	1,832	13

Source: Federal Reserve Bank of New York.

It is not a coincidence that the bank in question, the Bank of New
York, was owned by Bruce Rappaport; the 'familiar Swiss banker'
in whose Swiss bank account the Iran-Contra proceeds were
deposited along with the $500 million Saudi-Afghanistan fund
skimmed by the Reagan White House.

The article in *Veterans Today* concludes: *...It suggests that certain
key unknown figures in the Federal Reserve may have been in
collusion with key unknown figures at the Bank of New York to
create a situation where $240 billion in off balance sheet securities
created in 1991 as part of an official covert operation to overthrow
the Soviet Union, could be cleared without publicly acknowledging
their existence.* [bold, mine]

Bruce Rapport's Bank of New York along with the Federal Reserve
was at the very epicenter of the events behind 9/11. Once again,

153

gold, money and power were at stake and the bankers provided sufficient cover for the guilty to make sure no one knew what had happened; and no one did—at least not until the document that explained 9/11, *Collateral Damage*, appeared on the web.

ILLICIT POWER ILLICIT GOLD

The source material for the allegations in Veterans Today is a remarkable 58-page document, *Collateral Damage*, US Covert Operations and the Terrorist Attacks on September 11, 2001 attributed to "EP Heidner".

Heidner's document is a covert Rosetta Stone, shedding light on the hidden world of power and intrigue; where death and destruction are considered collateral damage. *Collateral Damage* not only confirms the role of gold as power, it reveals the pivotal role of Barrick Gold, now the world's largest gold mining company, in the laundering of China's stolen gold.

US Intelligence operations had been siphoning off the gold [China's stolen gold] *for three decades. However in 1986 Vice President George Bush took over the gold from Marcos and the gold was removed to a series of banks, notably Citibank, Chase Manhattan, Hong Kong Shanghai Banking Corporation, UBS and Banker's Trust, and held in a depository in Kloten, Switzerland.*

In 1992, George Bush served on the Advisory Board of Barrick Gold. The Barrick operation would create billions of dollars of paper gold by creating 'gold derivatives' …[and] *would become an investment for nearly every gold bullion bank associated with the Marcos gold recovery* [China's stolen gold]. *These banks would loan gold to Barrick, which would then sell the borrowed gold as derivatives, with the promise of replacing the borrowed gold with their gold mining operation.*

Barrick, which has no mining operations in Europe, used two refineries in Switzerland: MKS Finance S.A. and Argor-Heraeus S.A. – both on the Italian border near Milan, a few hours away from the gold depository in Zurich…The question that Barrick and other *banks needed to avoid answering is: <u>what gold was Barrick refining in Switzerland, as they have no mines in that region?</u>*

Barrick would become a quiet gold-producing partner for a number of major banks, and its activities became subject to an FBI investigation into gold-price-fixing. The records on this investigation were kept in the FBI office on the 23rd floor of the North Tower which was destroyed by bomb blasts shortly before the Tower collapsed.
p. 11, *Collateral Damage*: US Covert Operations and the Terrorist Attacks on September 11, 2001, EP Heidner (2008)

Heidner's full 58-page report explaining the motives behind 9/11 can be downloaded at: http://www.scribd.com/doc/9442970/Collateral-Damage-US-Covert-Operations-and-the-Terrorist-Attacks-on-September-11-200128062008

Collateral Damage contains information that the media has ignored, buried or denied. Today, societal control in America is maintained through the media. In the media, the American public—the unknowing, unwitting and gullible—read lies, half-lies and half-truths believing them to be fact. But to find the truth, especially where power's concerned, it's necessary to look hard, deep and elsewhere.

Deep Black Lies, the website of former UK banker, David Guyatt is such a place where one can find the dark truths that belie the claims of legitimate power proffered on behalf of those who rule.

Guyatt delves deeply into the dark machinations of power surrounding gold, money and power; and like Heidner's *Collateral Damage*, Guyatt's website, *Deep Black Lies*, provides answers to questions the powerful would wish to remain unasked and unanswered.

THE BANKER'S GRAVE

The victims of 9/11 are considered collateral damage by those who pursue gold, money and power to no other end. Howard Hughes' banker, Norman Thirion, was fortunate to have escaped with his life when he crossed the powerful elites who controlled the Reagan White House.

Other bankers, e.g. Roberto Calvi, Michele Sindona and Edmund Safra, were not so lucky. Roberto Calvi, former chairman of Banco Ambrosiano, was hung by the neck beneath Blackfriar's Bridge in London in 1982. Michele Sindona, former owner of Franklin National Bank, died after drinking coffee laced with arsenic in an Italian prison in 1986; and Edmond Safra, owner of Republic National Bank, burned to death barricaded and trapped in his heavily guarded penthouse in Monaco in 1999.

Each banker knew the secrets of the powerful who ultimately determined their interests were best served with the three bankers dead. Calvi and Sindona were murdered after their banks collapsed but Safra's death was different. Safra died with his financial empire intact—but, of the three, Safra's death was the most curious as the prosecution's explanation was both convoluted and unconvincing in the extreme.

The commonly-accepted—and highly improbable—version of Safra's death can be found at Wikipedia; where Safra's attorney alleged in court that Safra's killer, nurse and former Green Beret, Ted Maher, .. *did indeed start the fire in order to gain acceptance from Mr. Safra...He did not intend to kill Mr. Safra. He just wanted Mr. Safra to appreciate him more. He loved Mr. Safra.*

A far more plausible explanation for Safra's fiery demise is found at The Institute for the Study of Globalization and Covert Politics (ISGP) website regarding the secretive 1001 Club of which Safra was a member.

Edmond Safra, the late head of the New York-based Republic National Bank, gave evidence to the FBI concerning the diversion [of a $4.8 billion IMF "stabilization credit" for Russian that never reached those for whom it was intended] *...Geneva prosecutor Bertrand Bertossa* [maintains] *Safra was murdered for giving evidence to both the FBI and Swiss prosecutors concerning the* *diversion of the IMF credit..the US $4.8 billion credit went from the New York Federal Reserve Bank to* [Safra's] *Republic National Bank and then to various banks in Switzerland and elsewhere, but not to Russia...at the start of autumn 1999* [Russian oligarch] *Boris Berezovsky visited Safra at his estate in southern France. The two men.. had a three-hour conversation in "raised voices," after which Safra fled in a panic to his heavily fortified Monte Carlo residence* [where two months later he was burned to death in his penthouse.]

One year before his death, Safra's Republic Bank had also provided information to the FBI on Russian money-laundering activities at the Bank of New York [Bruce Rappaport's bank]. The night Safra was killed, Safra's Israeli-trained bodyguards were conveniently off-duty. Dead bankers don't talk.

THE 1001 CLUB

Edmond Safra was a member of The 1001 Club, a highly secretive organization founded by Prince Bernhard, the former president of the Bilderberg Group. The membership of The 1001 Club reads like a Who's Who of those on whose behalf the Bilderbergers toil.

When I came across the 1001 Club's membership list, I looked for Bruce Rappaport's name. Though not listed, Rappaport was mentioned in relationship to 1001 Club member, Dr. Alfred Hartmann, *Swiss gnome extraordinaire*, former director of Rothschild banking group and former high ranking executive at the notoriously corrupt bank, BCCI.

Dr. Hartmann's provenance makes Bruce Rappaport look like Mother Teresa. If Bruce Rappaport was a USB hub of covert criminality, illusory respectability and political sociopathy, Dr. Alfred Hartmann was an über-hub. David Whitby and Alan A. Block in *The Organized Criminal Activities of the Bank of Credit and Commerce*, BCCI, refer to Dr. Hartmann as follows:

6. [footnote] *Dr. Alfred Hartmann, director of Swiss Military Intelligence, former general manager of Union Bank of Switzerland and later chairman of Hoffman LaRoche. Hartmann resigned from*

La Roche following a price-fixing scandal involving the European Community...Main board director Rothschild family bank holding companies and general manager Rothschild A.G. Zurich. Resigned after payments by [Rothschild A.G. Zurich] *to the alleged assassins of Roberto Calvi (Banco Ambrosiano).....director of Intermaritime Bank (Bruce Rappaport), Royal Bank of Scotland (Switzerland). Hartmann was chairman of BCCI's audit committee (Luxembourg) but has never been investigated by the SFO (Serious Financial Office/Switzerland) or the FBI...*

45. [footnote] *Gold played an integral part in BCCI's money – laundering operations. BCCI gold dealings for Colombian drug cartels were passed through BCP (Banque de Commerce et de Placement) in association with Rothschild A.G. Zurich (Dr. Albert Hartmann).*

More on the activities of Dr. Hartmann is found at David Guyatt's *Deep Black Lies* website: *..Of more than passing interest in these matters is Dr. Alfred Hartmann, who had run the Banque de Commerce et de Placement (BCP), Geneva, for many years...large sums of money earned by .. market rigging activities were laundered through the BCP. Hartmann was also the Vice Chairman and General Manager of Rothschilds Bank A.G. and the vice president of the CIA connected Inter-Maritime Bank* [Bruce Rappaport's bank]. *The BCP is also said to have played a part in the Iran-Contra affair. This cannot come as any great surprise, for Hartmann was known as a long-term CIA asset. His contact or "controller" was none other than Edwin Wilson, the CIA operative who we earlier learned specialized in gay and pedophile blackmail stings against political targets...He is also known to have specialized in creating financial "fronts" for the CIA. Dr. Hartmann, meanwhile, would later become a senior executive in BCCI, the bank that provided a full service to drug lords, gun-runners, terrorists, gangsters and the US and European intelligence community.*

The information on The 1001 Club and Edmond Safra came from the Institute for the Study of Globalization and Covert Politics (ISGP). ISGP also has information on the highly secretive *Le Cercle*, a group composed of pan-European nationalists, white racists, extreme right-wing Catholics, and right-wing Americans, e.g. General Vernon Walters (suspected of involvement in the assassination of JFK), William Colby (Director of the CIA), William Casey (Director of the CIA, Chairman of the SEC and golfing buddy of Bruce Rappaport) etc.

For more information on *Le Cercle*, ISGP recommends reading *Rogue Agents* by David Teacher.
For free download, see http://mediafire.com/?2qvkx4nvdj9zyk6.

Another member of the exclusive 1001 Club—along with Edmond Safra, Dr. Alfred Hartmann and various Rothschilds, e.g. Baron Edmund de Rothschild, Baroness Nadine de Rothschild, Edmund L. de Rothschild, Baroness Guy de Rothschild, etc.—is the founder and chairman of Barrick Gold, Peter Munk.

The ostensible purpose of The 1001 Club is to raise funds and support the World Wildlife Foundation. Whether The 1001 Club is a true service organization or the Rotary Club for the Dark Side is unknown.

AMERICA, AMERICA
WHAT HAS BECOME OF THEE

The only difference between the killing of Trayvon Martin in Sanford, Florida and the US invasion of Iraq is scale. On February 26, 2012 Trayvon Martin was no more armed and no more a threat to George Zimmerman than on March 19, 2003 Iraq had weapons of mass destruction and was threatening the United States of America.

My generation came of age during the 1960s, an era of sex, drugs and rock 'n roll, fueled in no small part by LSD, the psychedelic elixir introduced to America by the CIA's ultra-secret MKULTRA program.

Personal note to the CIA for the introduction of LSD to the youth of America: Thanks!!!

Darryl Robert Schoon

Our generation's opposition to the Vietnam War, our support of civil rights for all—including blacks and women—and our desire for peace was considered by some to be un-American.

Un-American does not describe who or what we are nor does it in any way define America. Ronald Reagan's *ronin*, his errant cold-war warriors now deeply embedded in America's power structure hijacked America, depleted its financial resources and robbed the nation of its future…and 9/11…well, now *that's* un-American.

What happened on 9/11 constitutes high treason; and if America doesn't have the courage to demand the truth of those responsible at the point of imprisonment and death in a public forum, this once-great nation will suffer the fate of those who lack the courage to face their past in order to face their future.

QUIS CUSTODIET IPSOS CUSTODES
WHO WILL GUARD THE GUARDIANS

GOLD, MONEY & POWER

Some say gold is money
Some say gold is power
Some say gold will save us
In this troubled hour

But gold is more and sometimes less
Than man would wish it be
Only man creates his fate
A truth he cannot see

Man will not be saved
By silver or by gold
But that's a lesson man won't learn
Even when he's told

There's a truth that's in us all
More precious than pure gold
Love your neighbor as yourself
For this we have been told

The days ahead will darken soon
We'll need to learn to share
So value gold and silver
But remember how to care

Without the Light, there are no shadows

Cry not America for the loss
Of your freedoms and dreams
Why mourn them now
You who did not notice their absence before

Darryl Robert Schoon

Exhibit 1

Transglobal Productions Ltd Board of Directors
Robert E. Cushman Jr USMC ret, former Deputy Director CIA, Chairman
David D. C. MacKenzie, President
Dr. Jon Speller, Vice President & Secretary
Perry Morgan, Vice President & Treasurer
Rabbi Morton Rosenthal, Director
Muhammad Abdul-Rauf, Director

Transglobal Productions Ltd.

42ND FLOOR, 122 EAST 42ND STREET
NEW YORK, NEW YORK 10168
(212) 687-9300   (800) 221-2270

Board of Directors
Gen. Robert E. Cushman, Jr. USMC (Ret.)
Chairman
David D. C. MacKenzie
President
Dr. Jon P. Speller
Vice President and Secretary
Perry Morgan
Vice President and Treasurer
Rabbi Morton Rosenthal
Director
Muhammad Abdul-Rauf
Director

c/o International Banking Services
1301 Dove Street, Suite 400
Newport Beach, California 92660
(714) 851-1948
Telex: 183573 INTL BANK NPBH

February 15, 1983

Lord Cranbourne
No. 2 Swan Walk
London S.W. 3
ENGLAND

Dear Lord Cranbourne:

As I have been unexpectedly delayed here in California finalizing the paperwork for the financing request on our film project, "JIHAD," I thought it a good idea to drop you a note so you might be kept abreast of our plans.

As of this moment, Dr. Bernard Thirion (President of International Banking Services and former international banker to Howard Hughes) will be arriving in London during the week of February 21 in order to represent us in securing the commitment on our financing.

Although several capable entities have expressed a genuine interest in funding us, we intend to take every measure to insure a successful and speedy resolution. With the potential the 1984 Los Angeles Olympic games represent to our cause, it is essential that we be in release by the summer of 1984. We simply cannot afford to leave anything to chance that might cause us delay down the line.

Consequently, I have taken the liberty of giving Dr. Thirion your phone number as we want you to know more of our plans, and I am sure you will want to be of assistance if it is possible.

Until we next meet, I hope this finds you well. Thanking you in advance I remain

Yours sincerely,

TRANSGLOBAL PRODUCTIONS LTD.

Perry Morgen
Vice President

P.S. Enclosed is an article I thought you might find interesting.

cc: General Robert E. Cushman, Jr.
Dr. Bernard Thirion

Darryl Robert Schoon

Exhibit 2

Note reference to "private" American participation in budget request to Saudi Prince Bandar by General Cushman

DEPARTMENT OF ECONOMICS
(213) 743-2487

December 15, 1983

His Royal Highness Prince Bandar ibn Sultan
Ambassador
Royal Kingdom of Saudi Arabia
Washington, D.C.
Attention: His Excellency Ambassador Siraj

    Persuent to authorization by His Majesty the former King of
Afghanistan, I am attaching herewith our memorandom, "Support for
the Afghanistan Resistance Coalition," for consultation including
Budget I, Budget II, and a proposal by General Cushman for private
American participation.

    I look forward to hearing from you for the purpose of
discussing this memorandum.

    With highest personal esteem, I remain

                Sincerely yours,

                Nake M. Kamrany

UNIVERSITY OF SOUTHERN CALIFORNIA, UNIVERSITY PARK - MC 0035, LOS ANGELES, CALIFORNIA 90089-0035

Exhibit 3

Handwritten note by British Viscount Lord Cranbourne describing ties between groups supporting the Afghan resistance

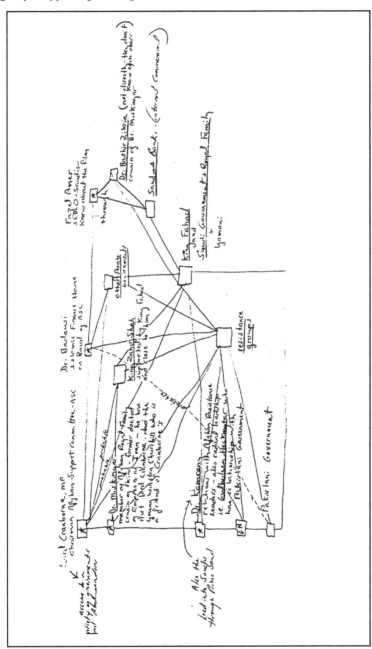

Darryl Robert Schoon

Exhibit 3

Letter from General Cushman to Norman Thirion informing him that Ronald Sablosky is replacing him as Transglobal's financial representative

12318 Firth of Tae Dr
Fort Washington,Md 20744

26 Dec 1983

Dr. B. N. Thirion
By hand of Ronald Sablosky

Dear Norman:

    I have sent this letter with Ronald Sablosky to confirm that I have authorized him to represent me and our group. Since he has far better understanding of financial matters than I do, he has been assigned the task of verifying all of our representations to his satisfaction.

    I have given him full-authority to consult with and utilize any of his banking contacts that he feels might be of value to our project.

    We are quickly approaching our moment of truth and I know you believe as I do that every effort must be made to insure a total success for all of us.

Sincerely,

R . E. Cushman, Jr
General, U. S. Marine Corps (Retired)

Books by Darryl Robert Schoon

Light in a Dark Place – The Prison Years (2006, 2nd Ed. 2012)
Darryl Robert Schoon's stories, poetry and essays are political, spiritual, always human and, at times, enlightened. "Darryl's voice is one that at times seems to tap into the very soul of the universe" (Marshall Thurber, founder of the Positive Deviant Network). *Light in a Dark Place* tells the story of Howard Hughes' banker who gave details of a Reagan White House skim of Saudi funds. The funds were discovered in a CIA Swiss bank account controlled by an Israeli banker later linked to 9/11. These links shed light on why 9/11 happened.

Time of the Vulture: How to Survive the Crisis and Prosper in the Process (2007, 2009, 3rd Ed. 2012)
This book predicted in 2007 why an economic crisis of unexpected magnitude and consequences was about to occur and was updated in 2012. Bought by readers in 25 countries, e.g. the US, UK, Australia, China, Switzerland, France, Paraguay, etc., it explains the nature of the crisis and ways to survive and profit.

You Can't Always Get What You Want – a novel (2012)
"Who do you think you are anyhow? At least I know I'm in a cage." The words of the monkey are never forgotten as the protagonist pursues dreams of romance on his way to Paris in a tension-filled novel of intrigue, danger and deception.

Is God Confused? – thoughts on the human condition (2012)
God isn't confused. Man is confused. This book explains mankind's predicament and the solution. Darryl Robert Schoon's spiritual observations on life are as uniquely penetrating as his observations about bankers and money.

The Way to Heaven – thoughts on the human condition (2012)
The way to heaven isn't easy but it's a lot easier than staying as you are; and the sooner you start, the sooner you'll arrive. Judgments will keep us in hell; forgiveness will lead us to heaven.

These books can be ordered at **www.drschoon.com**.

Made in United States
Orlando, FL
16 August 2022

21084144R00098